FANTASY LITERATURE
in the Elementary Classroom

Strategies for Reading, Writing, and Responding

FANTASY LITERATURE

in the Elementary Classroom

Strategies for Reading, Writing, and Responding

by Monica Edinger

SCHOLASTIC
PROFESSIONAL **B**OOKS

NEW YORK • TORONTO • LONDON • AUCKLAND • SYDNEY

To all my students

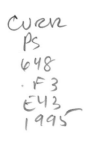

Cover design by Vincent Ceci and Frank Maiocco
Interior design by Solutions by Design, Inc.
Cover illustration by Scott Wright

ISBN 0-590-25110-4

Printed in the U.S.A.

1 2 3 4 5 6 7 8 9 10   14   02 01 00 99 98 97 96 95

Table of Contents

5 VISUALIZING FANTASY: A STUDY OF *ALICE IN WONDERLAND* AND ITS ILLUSTRATORS 69

6 BOOK INTO FILM: A COMPARATIVE STUDY OF *THE WONDERFUL WIZARD OF OZ*—BAUM'S BOOK AND THE MGM MOVIE 85

7 READING FANTASY LITERATURE ALOUD. 101

8 FANTASY LITERATURE IN AN INDEPENDENT READING PROGRAM 107

ACKNOWLEDGMENTS

It was my fantasy as a child to see my name on a book when I grew up. I became a teacher and enjoyed focusing my creative energies in my classroom for my students, never expecting my dream to come true. Thanks to Adrienne Schure, Terry Cooper, and Helen Moore Sorvillo of Scholastic for making it happen.

The National Endowment for the Humanities provided me with summers of scholarship in 1990 at Princeton University, 1992 at the Bank Street College of Education, and in 1993 at the University of Rochester. Ulrich Knoepflmacher started me thinking about new ways of bringing literature to my students, Judy Pasamanick brought me into contact with others interested in fantasy literature, and Russell Peck inspired me beyond measure to search for *Cinderella* far beyond the usual places.

I am grateful to Peter Stillman, my honest writing instructor at Northeastern University's 1994 Summer Writing Institute at Martha's Vineyard and my thoughtful and sensitive response group.

This book would not exist without the support and inspiration that I received from the Dalton School community.

I am especially grateful to Peter Sommer who encouraged me and cheered me on.

Thank you to my family, especially my father, a writer-scholar and an inspiration to me always.

Finally, my greatest thanks to Daniel Kramarsky who has helped me at every step of the way, from casual conversations on fantasy in the classroom to being my first and most important reader.

Introduction

"Do you believe in Dorothy?" five-year-old Adele asked her father.

"Of course I do," he replied. "Not only was she in the movie and story, but she is in many other stories that we can invent." And so they did, creating new adventures for the plucky heroine of *The Wizard of Oz*.

"You see," said Adele, "she continues to live in our stories."

We accept children's enjoyment and involvement with fantasy as they begin school, less so as they grow older. Somehow the cozy story time readings of fantasy picture books give way to the private solitudinal studying of textbooks. As school gets more serious, classroom literature gets more realistic. Adults want to be sure that children are able to distinguish fantasy from reality, that they don't use fantasy to escape from reality. Yet, even the most level-headed child will continue to seek out the fantastical, reading it through adolescence and into adulthood, on her own if the school doesn't provide it. Whether we like it or not, fantasy is alive and well in video games, cartoons, and comics. Bookstores are full of fantasy literature for adults and children. Teachers of all ages need to tap into this appeal and welcome Dorothy and her peers into the stories of their classrooms.

This book will introduce you to the possibilities of fantasy literature. Included is background information on folktales, fairy tales, novels, and authors as well as practical language arts activities to use with your own class. My approach is thematic and multidimensional embracing reading, writing, speaking, and the visual and performing arts. The units are tried and true; I have developed and used them with elementary students over a number of years. While my experience has been mainly with fourth graders, the units are adaptable for younger and older students. Use the ideas in this book as a stepping-off point, change them and mold them to fit your style of teaching and your students' particular needs.

CHAPTER 1

An Introduction to Fantasy Literature in the Classroom

Imagination is more important than knowledge.

ALBERT EINSTEIN, "ON SCIENCE"

hen I was in elementary school, my family spent a year in a rented house in St. Louis. It was big and old, similar to the house in the film *Meet Me in St. Louis*, full of musty books. My favorite place was a vestibule that contained the complete works of Dickens and all of Baum's Oz books. I spent that year happily moving back and forth between the ultrarealism of Dickensian England and the extravagant fantasies of Oz. Both presented worlds of escape with characters and situations that fascinated me. Some fantasy worlds were so vivid that my friends and I tried to make them real: after reading Mary Norton's *The Borrowers* we created tiny homes just perfect for the little people that might come, and the whole backyard became Neverland thanks to James M. Barrie's *Peter Pan*.

So it was only natural for me to bring fantasy literature to my students when I became a teacher. Fairy tales are perfect for teaching predictable story structure, and a novel like *Alice in Wonderland* ideal for a unit on illustration. Imaginary worlds are ripe environments for stimulating creativity—mine and my students'. Most importantly, fantasy is a way to tap into children's immediate concerns. Issues of vital importance to them, friendship, honesty, right and wrong, are central to this type of literature.

WHAT IS FANTASY LITERATURE?

There may be as many definitions of fantasy literature as there are definers. J.R.R. Tolkien (1966), author of *The Hobbit,* defines the fairy-story as "one which touches on or uses Faerie, whatever its own main purpose may be: satire, adventure, morality, fantasy." He is ruthless in his exceptions: *Gulliver's Travels* is out because "Such tales report many marvels, but they are marvels to be seen in this mortal world in some region of our own time and space; distance alone conceals them" as is *Alice in Wonderland* since he "would also exclude, or rule out of order, any story that uses the machinery of Dream, the dreaming of actual human sleep, to explain the apparent occurrence of its marvels" (p. 13) and beast-fables "in which no human being is concerned; or in which the animals are the heroes and heroines, and the men and women, if they appear, are mere adjuncts; and above all those in which the animal form is only a mask upon a human face. . . ." (p. 15) On the other hand, Lloyd Alexander (1984) claims that "All art, by definition of the word, is fantasy in the broadest sense. . . .I suppose you might define realism as fantasy pretending to be true; and fantasy as reality pretending to be a dream." (p. 143) Laurence Yep (1987) sees "science fiction as fantasy in new forms . . . of fantasy and writing in general as a special way of seeing. It's a way of looking at the world more intensely and more sensitively and more sharply than we normally would." (p. 10)

So, of course, here is my own, somewhat modest definition of fantasy literature: a narrative that is simply not possible in real life. This includes magic, mythological creatures such as dragons, aliens from who knows where, imaginary worlds and even (sorry, J.R.R. Tolkien) talking animals and stories framed in dreams. However, there is more to the fantasy story than magic and imaginary landscapes. These stories get to the heart of what we most value: the triumph of good over evil, the importance of love, and the virtues of truth, honor, courage. Through the filter of a fantasy world, we are better able to understand our own. "And yet . . . and yet the talking beasts, the ballet of birch and oak, the riders of the wind are another way of presenting the real world. And the reader—child or adult—who learns to use eyes and ears and mind and heart in this manner can never again look at the world in a one-dimensional way." (Yolen, 1981, p. 62)

FROM TELLING TO READING TO VIEWING

Fantasy literature came out of the folkloric tradition. Long before books there were storytellers holding audiences of adults and children spellbound with tales of magical exploits. Peasants outwitted giants, animals acted like humans, and princes saved princesses from dragons. In 1697, the Frenchman Charles Perrault wrote a very successful collection of fairy tales based on the old tales of storytellers. Translated, they were exported to England and America and became enormously popular. Even today the Perrault stories are quintessential fairy tales for many of us. The versions of "Cinderella" and "Little Red Ridinghood" that we know best are Perrault's. German versions of both these tales and many more were collected by the Grimm brothers and published in a nineteenth-century collection of fairy tales. "Rapunzel," "Hansel and Gretel," and "Snow White" are well-known Grimm tales. Others have collected and produced published fairy tale collections, but Perrault's and the Grimms' are the most well known.

The first published fairy tales were based on the traditional oral tales. Their success inspired authors like Hans Christian Anderson to write original tales such as "The Little Mermaid" and "The Ugly Duckling." Lewis Carroll's *Alice in Wonderland* is an example of the book-length story, also known as a literary fairy tale. Carroll and L. Frank Baum, author of the Oz books, were interested in creating contemporary stories with real heroines and heroes, "modern" fairy tales, as Baum put it. Alice and Dorothy are not princesses from a past time, but very real, very normal little girls. The enormous success of such works encouraged others to write fantasy novels for children. One of the most popular authors of this sort of story is Roald Dahl. Stories like *Charlie and the Chocolate Factory* and *James and the Giant Peach* combine fantastical elements (the giant peach and insects) and magic (the workings of Mr. Wonka within his chocolate factory) with the realistic hardships of small mistreated children. Just as poor peasant children outwitted evil witches in the old tales, so does the title character in *Matilda* triumph over the Trunchbull, her evil headmistress.

Today, fantasy is alive and well in all forms of media. Animated films, from Saturday morning television cartoons to the more complex features of Disney, have been children's staples for years. What are Batman and Superman but newer princes, armed with magic in the form of their special powers, out to slay dragons like the Joker or Lex Luthor. Video games are full of fantasy imagery. The tremendous growth of the computer industry in recent years is also stimulating new fantasy experiences. Popular programs exist that allow the user to create his or her own imaginary world. Yet whatever the vehicle, the old basic elements of the fantasy story remain constant: wickedness stamped out, the triumph of good, honor and truth upheld.

MULTICULTURAL FANTASY

Fantasy stories exist throughout the world. Dragons are prominent in China while genies are magical figures of the Middle East. Fantastic elements and narratives often originate in one place and then filter into other cultures which make them their own. We have African Cinderellas, the European Saint George and the Dragon, even American television's *I Dream of Jeannie*. No one "owns" these old stories and characters, which is why we see them used in every form, from opera to cartoons. They come out of an oral tradition and are used however the storytellers, authors, and artists wish. Some scholars claim that these ancient narratives are universal, archetypal stories that are simply repeated again and again in different forms.

Today in schools, traditional fantasy stories are frequently used to learn about other cultures. A unit on China is enriched by a reading of *Yeh Shen*, a Chinese Cinderella variant. John Steptoe's *Mufaro's Beautiful Daughters* becomes a vehicle for a study of Africa. With our concern for broadening the content in our classrooms to include many cultures, using fantasy tales in this way seems perfect. Yet some caution is in order. Folktales, while they might originate in a specific place, are constructs of the teller. Each teller and author places his or her own biases, cultural orientations, and interests in the tale. An American retelling of an Asian tale is not the same as an Asian telling of the tale no matter how carefully researched. Folktales are slippery artifacts as they can equally mirror and oppose cultural norms. And after all, magic is not a real life way to solve problems. Teachers and students need to be conscious of this as they study these retellings.

WHY USE FANTASY LITERATURE IN THE CLASSROOM?

1. Fantasy literature comes out of the traditions and common culture of our society. E. D. Hirsch (1987) argues that we need to teach certain basic facts to our children so that they have a common cultural base. Of course, exactly what these facts are has been hotly debated for years. While I am uncomfortable with Hirsch's lists of must-knows, I must agree with him that children "need to understand elements in our literary and mythic heritage that are often alluded to without explanation. . . ." (p. 30) Traditional literature, in particular, is something with which all our students should be familiar. Folktales and fairy tales underlie much of later literature, and references to them abound in our day-to-day speech. We put students at a distinct disadvantage if we do not expose them to these stories.

2. Fantasy literature stimulates the imagination and encourages creativity. It is an excellent resource in the classroom to encourage original work. When our educational system is compared to the Japanese system, we admire their discipline, their ability to study hard and to work cooperatively. However, they admire our ability to foster creative thinking in our schools, to help our students develop original ideas. Fantasy literature is an ideal vehicle for bringing out creative thinking in children.

3. Fantasy literature encourages an interdisciplinary approach. Children instinctively wish to respond to fantasy in kind, using a wide variety of media. It is easy to include the visual and performing arts in a unit on fantasy. For some students storytelling, either through listening or telling, is the best avenue into literature. Math figures heavily in fantasy literature. Numbers are typically significant in folktales, and books such as *Alice in Wonderland* or Norton Juster's *The Phantom Tollbooth* are full of mathematical allusions. In social studies, myths and folktales can be one of many informational sources about a culture.

4. Fantasy literature is a fine tool for developing critical thinking skills. It is a genre that encourages wondering. Children are easily nudged to go beyond the literal, to speculate and muse about what is less obvious to the eye. They will quickly note the predictable quality of fairy tales and enjoy pointing out specific elements such as the symbolism of the number three, the contrast between rich and poor, the lesson or moral. Fantasy novels are often complex, requiring students to dig deep for true understanding.

5. Fantasy literature provides models to young writers. Children love to write fantasy. Often we discourage them from doing so because their stories are modeled on video games or comics. But we can provide children with good models and then guide them in the writing process. Too many teachers I know avoid this genre in their writing workshops because they feel their students produce pages upon pages of poorly written fantasy narrative; that they can't control it. Studying fantasy stories as models for writing can help writing workshop leaders and students focus more comfortably on the genre.

6. Fantasy literature provides a readily viable ethical dimension in the classroom. These are stories of good and

CHILDREN'S VOICES ON FANTASY

Jody: I like fantasy literature because like usually when I come back from gymnastics I'm very tired and grouchy. But when I sit back and read a fantasy book it kind of gets me out of a grouchy mood because it makes me put all that just went on out of my head so that I can relax!!!!!!!

Anna: I love fantasy literature because it makes me fall asleep and really drift off to *that place.* . . . I like to be read to more than ever . . . sometimes at night I beg my mom to read one more chapter.

Mack: I do like writing fantasy because anything can happen. You can fly with fantasy.

Sarah: I love writing fantasy books because I don't limit myself to any amount of silliness or magic happenings. I just go along and the ideas just develop in my head as I write.

---

evil; basic virtues are at the heart of these tales. The literature can be used to provide a moral stance in the classroom. Sometimes fantasy literature is a safer, less threatening way to reflect on personal hardships and dilemmas. For some, it is easier to consider moral issues within the context of an imaginary world rather than in a world too much like the real one.

CONCLUSION

I use fantasy literature in my classroom for many reasons. It is there to make children wonder, to feed their imaginations, to develop their literary understandings, to make them creators and dreamers. Sometimes I use fantasy literature because I feel my students should have a foundation in traditional stories; sometimes, because I want them to explore tales from other cultures. At times, I will find reasons I wasn't aware of—perhaps a story will help a child better sort through a difficult family situation or deepen a student's understanding of honorable behavior. The important thing is that all these reasons are important; one does not take precedence over another.

REFERENCES

Alexander, Lloyd. (1984). "Wishful Thinking—or Hopeful Dreaming?" In Robert H. Boyer (Ed.) *Fantasists on Fantasy.* New York: Avon.

Hirsch, E. D. (1987). *Cultural Literacy.* Boston: Houghton Mifflin.

Tolkien, J.R.R. (1966). "On Fairy-Stories." In *The Tolkien Reader.* New York: Ballantine.

Yep, Laurence. (1987). "World Building." In Barbara Harrison and Gregory Maguire (Eds.) *Innocence & Experience: Essays and Conversations on Children's Literature.* New York: Lothrop, Lee & Shepard.

Yolen, Jane. (1981). *Touch Magic.* New York: Philomel.

CHAPTER 2

Literature Studies

Grace was a girl who loved stories.
She didn't mind if they were read to her
or told to her or made up in her own head.
She didn't care if they were in books or
movies or out of Nana's long memory.
Grace just loved stories.

MARY HOFFMAN, *AMAZING GRACE*

ooks have always been the cornerstone of my existence. I have rarely run the briefest errand without bringing along a book, and I am happiest on vacation with hours free to read. When I was a child, the highlight of my week was my visit to the library where I took out as many books as I could carry home. Once I attempted to copy a much beloved book by hand. (I managed three chapters, but eventually had to return it or risk losing borrowing privileges.) I treasured the books I owned, and family and friends always knew that the perfect gift for me was a book. My passion for reading and books has been something I have always communicated to my students throughout my twenty years of teaching.

Teachers have numerous lives, perhaps as many as cats. In addition to my life as a book lover, I have lives as world traveler, artist, and computer maven, all of which have contributed to my growth as a teacher. My most recent life began in the summer of 1990, at Princeton University, when I studied children's literature with Professor Uli Knoepflmacher as a National Endowment for the Humanities fellow. Life as a literary scholar was a new experience for me, and I studied children's literature with the same degree of seriousness that others do Shakespeare. There I was, discoursing on the meaning of *Charlotte's Web* at the seminar table and examining rare copies of *Alice in Wonderland* in the library. That fall I returned to my classroom excited about helping my students work as I had. Now, my students become literary experts as they develop their reading and writing skills through intensive experiences with a wide variety of literature.

Children As Literary Experts

My students come to me with varying degrees of abilities, comfort and attitudes about reading. Their previous school experiences have ranged from whole language to traditional classrooms. Some are avid readers and throw themselves into books. Others struggle, still locked into decoding issues, insecure and negative about books. My challenge is to create a learning environment that excites and empowers everyone.

Promoting the idea that we all can be literary experts helps to build a classroom community. Language arts skills such as reading, writing, listening, and speaking are all easy to nurture within such a literature based program. Since my class is heterogeneous, I am careful to vary whole class, small group, and individual book study. I also balance teacher-selected versus student-selected reading materials. Individual conferences and group discussions on specific reading strategies are ways I help those with difficulties. Tremendous emphasis is given to personal response and interpretation. Writing is often tied directly to reading via journal entries, fiction written in response to reading, and research report writing.

Reader Response

One way to help children become literary experts is to use a reader response approach to literature. Louise M. Rosenblatt, a pioneer in this field, describes two types of reading: aesthetic and efferent. An aesthetic reading is personal; each person will bring his or her own experiences to the text and each of these transactions will be unique. My

Charlotte's Web will be very different from your *Charlotte's Web*. At the other end of the continuum, is the efferent stance: reading for information. Our skimming of the daily newspaper is a good example of efferent reading. Aesthetic and efferent stances can occur at the same time. "We read for information, but we are also conscious of emotions about it and feel pleasure when the words we call up arouse vivid images that are rhythmic to the inner ear. Or we experience a poem but are conscious of acquiring some information about, say, Greek warfare. To confuse matters even further, we can switch stances while reading. Our present purpose and past experiences, as well as the text are factors in our choice of stance." (Rosenblatt, 1991, p. 445)

Reader response encourages my students to value their own transactions with books and to learn that it is possible for everyone in the class to have a different interpretation of the same book, all equally valid. Once they understand this they can begin to approach books as scholars, returning to the text to see what else is in it, considering how it compares to other books, to real life, to anything else they wish to explore.

Independent Reading

My students select their own books for a nightly reading assignment and respond to these readings in class discussions and in a journal. I require that the children read thirty minutes a night and find parents helpful in seeing that this is accomplished. Often children need help choosing the right books, finding the right place to read, and sticking with it for the full thirty minutes. Sometimes parents use a timer to see that the thirty minutes of reading is accounted for; others plan a timetable of specific chapters and pages. As I get to know the children, I am able to work in a partnership with each child and his or her parents to help them become better readers. For some students, all I have to do is pull a book off a shelf in our classroom library and say, "I think you would really enjoy this book." For others it can be a larger quest to find the right book and the right way to read at home. Sometimes a child may need to try several books and many different authors until one really clicks. I encourage children to stop reading books they don't like. There is no reason that I can see to struggle through to the end of a book one hates, especially if reading is an unpleasant activity in the first place.

LITERATURE STUDIES

I have created a series of thematic units built around books that I love and that I feel are valuable for children to know. My students become literary experts, studying these books and authors. This can mean researching an author's life, discovering historical information relevant to the book, or even reading literary criticism if there is interest. The idea of studying and responding to literature as a communal experience is an important element of the program. These children are not solitudinal scholars, each isolated in his or her own ivory tower. Their ideas, responses, and interpretations expand as they interact with each other, with me, and with the text.

MODELING LITERARY EXPERTISE

In my classroom, I am the experienced reader and scholar. My role is to model passion and enthusiasm for literature, to demonstrate how to think deeply about books, and to nudge and bring out similar behaviors in my students. I have had time to develop a critical stance while my students come to me as neophytes, amazed that there is more to reading a book than simply getting the main ideas. Teachers are literary experts already and need to model what that means for their students. "Teachers are the leading critics in the classroom; they point the way to searching out the potential of a text." (Peterson and Eeds, 1990, p. 23) My students value my expertise even as they develop their own.

CREATING A CLASSROOM READING COMMUNITY

My students are used to a clearly defined system of weaker, better, and best readers. It is a struggle to get them to consider everyone as part of the same community of readers. They know which members of the class are avid readers who read a book a day and which ones struggle to get through a page a day. Some stumble along when reading orally, yet understand beautifully when left to read on their own. Others can decode every word, yet understand little of the subtleties of the text. Students quickly figure out "school" and have rock solid ideas as to what constitutes a good or bad reader. For them it has more to do with speed and accuracy than with personal response and interpretation.

To begin building a community of readers, I give my students the following letter the first week of school. We read and discuss it together.

Creating a whole-class community of readers is a way of breaking down the students' stereotypes of good and bad readers. I expect everyone to be responsible and capable of participating in our literature studies. For example, I put the responsibility on the children to decide how long they need to complete a book rather then

September 12, 1994

Dear Readers,

I would like to welcome you to our fourth grade reading club and tell you about what you can expect to be doing in Reading Workshop this year. I love to read and have been reading for a long time. But I didn't always love reading. I spent second grade in Germany. When I started school in Germany, I didn't like reading at all. This was a problem because I was learning to read German at school and English at home (with my mother). At some point that year something clicked and I began to like reading. My favorite book (which I have here in school) was *My Naughty Little Sister*. I also have my German reading book from that year. Every since then I have loved reading and have read all kinds of things, everything from Nancy Drew mysteries to *Tom Sawyer*.

Now I am sure you all have different feelings about reading. Some of you may love it, some may think it is okay, some may think it is boring, some may absolutely hate it. Well, whatever you think about reading it is something you need to do well because you will be doing it a lot in your life! There are so many reasons to read, and I hope that you will all identify many of them this year.

We will generally have Reading Workshop every day. There will be two aspects to the Reading Workshop. One part will involve your independent reading and the other will involve group literature study. You will not be assigned permanent reading groups. Some of your work will be independent, some in small groups, some with the whole class. The groups will change and be determined in different ways: by book choice, by numbering off, by who works well together, by talkers and listeners.

You will be expected to always have an independent reading book in school and for homework. You are expected to read this book at least thirty minutes every night and to bring it to school every day. Once a week you will be required to write about this book in your reading journal. I will write responses to your journal entries. I need to be able to read these entries, but you should not worry about spelling or punctuation. I am most interested in what you write, rather than how it looks. You may read whatever you wish. Your parents, classmates, the librarians, and I will be most willing to suggest books to read. In addition to writing about your reading in a journal, you will have conferences with me about your reading and, at times, discuss your reading in class meetings.

The other part of Reading Workshop will be literature study. We will be studying authors and their books as a class. You will be working as literary experts, studying books as do people in universities and colleges. For example, our first major study will be on E. B. White and our first book, *Charlotte's Web.* Many of you will already know White's books, but, believe me, this will be a new and different way of looking at them!

I love to read, love children's literature, and love leading literature studies. Every year it is so exciting to watch my class become a community of readers, learning to appreciate what everyone has to offer in the reading of a book.

Welcome to a wonderful, exciting year of reading and literature!

Ms. Edinger

imposing my own deadlines for them. Starting the year with a book like *Charlotte's Web* helps to quickly solidify the community. It is so well liked and well known that my fourth graders all feel confident about expressing their feelings about it to the group and to me in their journals.

In order to develop a true reading community I feel that I must help children move away from a good/bad view of readers. It is something that needs to be constantly reaffirmed as the year goes on. With every new unit, I am careful to stress the importance of deep understanding and personal response over speed and informational reading.

DISCUSSIONS

Discussions are a good way to help children think like scholars. I feel that I can learn a great deal about a book as I talk with others about it in a group. "Learning what others have made of a text can greatly increase such insight into one's own relationship with it. A reader who has been moved or disturbed by a text often manifests an urge to talk about it, to clarify and crystallize his sense of the work. He likes to hear other's views. Through such interchange he can discover how people bringing different temperaments, different literary and life experiences to the text have engaged in very different transactions with it." (Rosenblatt, 1976, p. 146)

Functioning as a discussion leader is one of the hardest things I do as a teacher. Generally, I begin with the question "What did you think of the book?" and move the discussion on from the initial responses. I must encourage all ideas, see that no one child or gender dominates the discussion, get everyone to participate, affirm the literal as well as the more abstract idea, know when to sit back and listen and when to step

in, model discomfort and confusion, encourage disagreement as a way of struggling with deeper meaning, move the discussion on with a new thought if necessary, pick up on ideas that demand more thought, and try throughout to observe my students' process. It is quite a juggling act! Yet, I have concluded after years of observation and contemplation about my role that I must be there, actively leading the discussion for the ideas to bubble up, be recognized, and examined.

JOURNALS

Journals are another means for my students and me to interact around a text. These are personal journals, also known as response journals, dialogue journals, or learning logs. Their purpose is to provide a private place for students to write responses to their reading and for me to respond back to them. When it works well, the journal becomes a private conversation between me and the student. At first, children respond to their independent reading. To help them get started, I read responses from former students and give them a list of response ideas, some from experts like Nancy Atwell; others, ideas that students and I have come up with over the years. The tendency is for responses to be plot summaries. As the year goes on, I am able to move most children away from these into more thoughtful responses. I have journal readings when each child selects a favorite entry to read to the class. Once we are involved in a literature study I will often ask children to respond to a specific book or film. Some children are able to express themselves more honestly in a journal while others, being more verbal, prefer the discussions.

The journal is a good way for children to distinguish writing to learn from writing for publication. I see the journals as reflective writing, primarily used to learn more. My responses to students' entries have to be as sensitive as my responses are in discussions. My students need to feel we are having a private dialogue and look forward to reading my responses as much as I look forward to reading theirs. Just as a child can find too many questions from me tedious, so can I let them know when they have bored me with endless plot summaries.

As the year goes on, we are able to begin comparing and contrasting books. After our *Cinderella* Study, for example, children will constantly refer back to it in their journals. They love comparing characters from different books, trying to see similarities and differences. Different classes have different interests. One year, I had a group that watched a great deal of television and brought that into their book discussions. Another group enjoyed writing letters on behalf of characters. Of course I had to answer the character not the student!

Every year I find journals to be a more powerful teaching tool. At first I called them "reading journals," but now I call them "response journals." That way we can use them to respond to whatever we wish. I use them for spontaneous responses to current events and to classroom problems, as well as to academic materials.

ORAL READINGS

hen I first began teaching fourth grade at my current school, we had homogeneous reading groups and I had my students read aloud every day. I was sure that it helped with comprehension, and it reassured me that they were all decoding correctly. Since we eliminated reading groups several years ago, students have made clear to me how much they disliked oral reading and how it only confused them rather than helped them. It helped me realize that fluent oral reading does not

necessarily make for perfect comprehension or vice versa. Therefore, I eliminated round robin reading and emphasized silent reading.

Last year I asked students to prepare favorite readings to present during our morning meetings. Two or three children read aloud every morning at the close of our meeting. The children loved explaining why they had selected a particular part of a book and read with wonderful expression and enjoyment. The others equally enjoyed listening. What made it different from round robin readings was that this time the children decided what to read and had a chance to practice beforehand. We weren't doing it to be sure everyone understood. We were doing it to hear what they liked. It made the experience completely different and enjoyable for all.

Serendipitously, poetry readings also have become part of our day. I run a very brief class meeting before dismissal where homework and issues of the day are discussed. One day last year a child came in with a book of Robert Frost's poetry and said she had been reading some of the poems with her father and wanted to read one to the class. I suggested she do so at the end of the day. The next day another child brought in a poem to read and before long we had established the end-of-day meeting as a time for poetry. I brought in a variety of poetry books and children searched the library for favorites. One of the most impressive was a child who did a remarkable reading of Poe's "The Raven" without any practice. There is no doubt that end-of-day poetry readings will become a permanent ritual in my classroom from now on.

WRITING

PERSONAL WRITING

Personal writing is the reflective, intimate kind that takes place in response journals. This is writing to learn, to muse and speculate. My students write to me in their journals with the understanding that I only wish to know more about their thinking. I make it clear that as long as I can read what they have written, handwriting and spelling do not matter.

PUBLIC WRITING

Public writing is for publication. Parents, teachers, and peers can all be readers of public writing. It can be a poem, a report, a story, or a poster. The important thing is that there is an understanding on the author's part that others will read this piece of writing. This means that drafts and revisions are an important part of the process of writing for publication. In my classroom we publish regularly: research journals, informational handbooks, book reviews, poetry posters, memoir books, and story collections.

Writing workshop in my class is a daily affair. I begin with mini-lessons based on the needs of my students and then have them write for the bulk of the period. Children confer with me and each other as they write and revise their pieces. The idea of multiple drafts is an important one for my students. Skills are taught in context: quotation marks, for example, become a mini-lesson topic when children are writing a lot of dialogue and find the skill useful. Whole class response sessions are a regular part of the workshop. Ten years ago I attended Lucy McCormick Calkin's Writing Institute at Teachers College Columbia University and have continued to learn about process writing through conferences, journals, workshops, and books. The writings of Donald Graves and Nancy Atwell have been especially influential in helping me grow as a writing teacher.

PROJECTS

One of the favorite ways to respond to literature is through projects. These are nothing new. I remember doing dioramas and posters when I was a child. They are still an excellent way for children to create an original and personal response to literature.

Numerous books exists with fine project ideas. Children love to write sequels and parodies, poems, and plays based on favorite works of literature. My students have done skits, puppet shows, raps, videos, and meals as projects. We have done whole class projects such as plays, murals, or magazines. Sometimes everyone works in groups and sometimes everyone works alone. Presenting projects is important. Children are thrilled to invite another class or, best of all, family members to a project presentation.

CONCLUSION

Elementary school children are capable of great interpretative depth when analyzing a piece of literature. Empowering children as literary experts is a way to encourage reflective thinking about books. In a heterogeneous reading community my students begin to deepen their ideas of what a good reader is, to understand that it is more than just the ability to read quickly, to get the facts. As the expert scholar, I model passion for reading and ways to interpret literature. By the end of the school year, my students need no encouragement to look for depth in the books they are reading; making connections has become a natural part of their reading process.

REFERENCES

Atwell, Nancy. (1987). *In the Middle.* Portsmouth, NH: Heinemann.

Hoffman, Mary. (1991). *Amazing Grace.* Illustrated by Caroline Binch. New York: Dial.

Peterson, Ralph, and Maryann Eeds. (1990). *Grand Conversations: Literature Groups in Action.* Toronto, Canada: Scholastic.

Rosenblatt, Louise M. (1991). "Literature - S.O.S." *Language Arts*, 68.

Rosenblatt, Louise M. (1978). *The Reader the Text the Poem.* Carbondale and Edwardsville: Southern Illinois University Press.

CHAPTER 3

TALKING ANIMALS: An Author Study of E. B. White

*I haven't told why I wrote the book,
but I haven't told why I sneeze, either.
A book is a sneeze.*

E. B. WHITE ON *CHARLOTTE'S WEB*

y sister and I frequently dressed our stoical cat in doll clothes and wheeled her about in a carriage. She was the baby in our games of House. Had our dogs been smaller and more cooperative I have no doubt we would have found roles for them, perhaps as beasts of burden or as additional family members. Stuffed animals also served as participants in a wide range of games. We provided them with food and clothing and used them in elaborate stories. My teddy bear stood by me when I was sent to my room, understood when everyone else was being unfair, and protected me against all the evils of the night.

Animals have a special place in our childhood. Perhaps it is their vulnerability, their reliance on us which parallels our needs as children. How else to explain the delight we take in animal stories, especially talking animal stories. Life in these books seems so real: the main characters act, feel, and suffer as human beings. Often they live in towns, hold jobs, or go to school. Even if the setting is an animal habitat, the characters in this genre act and speak as humans.

Certainly, a master of this genre was E. B. White. His three children's books, all featuring talking animals, are classics of children's literature. There is a timelessness to them that keeps them beloved by generation upon generation of children. A master writer and editor, White was meticulous about his work. An author study of E. B. White, centered around *Stuart Little, Charlotte's Web,* and *Trumpet of the Swan,* can be a fine way to help children appreciate what the art of writing is all about. It can also be a gentle entry into the world of fantasy literature.

STARTING THE YEAR
WITH E. B. WHITE

I begin the school year with this unit for several reasons. My students generally are already familiar with White's children's stories, and re-experiencing them is comforting at a time when everything else is so new. Not only are my fourth graders starting a new school year with a new teacher and a new class, but they are also in a new building as the first grade of our middle school. To make it even harder, our high school is in the same building. It is truly frightening for many of my small charges to move through the stairwells and halls, alternately ignored, teased, or belittled by their far older and larger schoolmates. It is easy for them to sympathize with Stuart's difficulties or identify with Wilbur, the runt of his litter.

Another reason to begin the year with E. B. White is that there is no better writer to present to children when teaching about writing process. White was one of the most accomplished writers and editors of this century. His enduring popularity ensures that there will always be plenty of material about his life and his writing, and especially about the writing of his children's books. Students realize that the magic of *Charlotte's Web* came from White's love of nature, meticulous research, pondering, and careful craftsmanship as a writer. It is a lesson that will stay with them forever.

White's books are also a very gentle introduction to fantasy literature. They hardly seem like other kinds of fantasy literature since the settings are so realistically rendered. I taught these books for years without thinking of them as fantasy literature. It was only when I began to think seriously about what fantasy literature was that I realized that talking animals like Stuart, Charlotte, and Louise belonged to the genre. These kinds of realistic talking animal stories are sometimes referred to as low fantasy while those with magic and imaginary lands are termed high fantasy. I have found that talking animal stories often appeal to children who dislike the higher types of fantasy literature.

CHARLOTTE'S WEB:
A WHOLE CLASS READING A
WHOLE BOOK TOGETHER

I begin the unit with a whole class study of *Charlotte's Web*. I do this because I simply think the book is one of the most perfect books ever written and my students invariably agree with me. *Charlotte's Web* was actually White's second children's book, a middle child, written after *Stuart Little* and before *Trumpet of the Swan*.

To begin, I seat my class in a circle on the floor of our meeting area and give each of them their own paperback copy of the book. I tell them that we will be studying the book as scholars do and that they will want to mark up the book with their own ideas—ending up with a very personal *Charlotte's Web*. I show them my marked-up, well-thumbed copy as an example. We discuss previous experiences with the book. For many, it was read to them. Others know the story from the animated film. A smaller number may have read it in school or on their own. Once in a while I come across a total neophyte and envy his or her pleasure as a first timer. In the course of the discussion, I introduce the idea of multiple readings of a book. This is a new idea for fourth graders. So many are still uncertain about reading; it is hard work for them and not always pleasurable. Reading a chapter book all the way through is a feat for many and the idea of rereading is revolutionary. Yet *Charlotte's Web* is so beloved that even the most reluctant readers are willing to approach it for the first, second, or umpteenth time. I tell them that I read it at least once every year (when they do) and enjoy it each time.

The idea that everyone in the class will be reading the same book is often new to many of my students. Their previous school reading experiences have tended to be in small groups. Often, the reading ability in the class will range from those who can read the book in a couple of hours to those who will need several weeks to complete it. I acknowledge this situation to the whole class immediately. They need to recognize this range among themselves and be sensitive and helpful to each other. We negotiate a date when everyone in the class feels they can be finished with the book. Generally, I have found that three weeks is a reasonable time for all. The book has twenty-two chapters, so a slow reader can plan to read approximately one chapter a day to meet such a deadline. Since I also have an independent reading program, children who finish quickly can continue with books of their own choice. For these children, the fear is that they will have forgotten the book in two weeks since they are used to reading small amounts and discussing it immediately within a reading group. It is another small lesson for these high achievers to realize that it is possible to read a book and still remember it weeks later (if it is worth remembering like *Charlotte's Web*).

I provide enough daily reading time so that everyone has plenty of time to finish the book. While I enjoy informal conversations about the book as children are reading it, I do not run formal whole group discussions until the everyone has finished the book. For years I taught reading by chapters. That is, I assigned a chapter to read and we discussed it the next day. I was always frustrated because I knew the whole book, but I couldn't discuss anything past the chapter we were on. Invariably, there were others in the group who had also read

further. It always struck me as a very artificial way to approach a book, and I have done away with it completely.

Certainly, my students are welcome to talk to each other and to me as they read the book. And they do. I listen to them read bits aloud that they like and discuss how they cried when Charlotte died. I watch those who become so absorbed in the book that it takes three calls from me until they look up and realize that it is time for gym. Weekly journal entries are all about the book: what they feel about it, who they like and don't like, and (for first timers) what they think will happen next.

FIRST RESPONSE DISCUSSIONS

When everyone is finished with the book, we meet as a whole class to give initial reactions. This is a very free-flowing discussion. I simply begin by asking, "What did you think of the book?" Invariably, someone will have something to say which will give someone else an idea and the discussion will be underway. I am strict about respect and courtesy. I am the discussion leader and require that everyone raise his or her hand in order to speak and listen respectfully to peers. If there are a lot of hands in the air I will call on several, "First Mary, then Jon, then Nancy, and then David." Running such a discussion with a large group is difficult. However, I feel that these discussions need to be with the whole class. It is still the beginning of the year and these children need to become a group. Discussing *Charlotte's Web* as a whole class is a way towards that goal. They need to hear each others' ideas and learn that Mary, who took three weeks to finish the book, has some of the most profound thoughts on the book. Mary also needs to realize that, despite being a slow reader, she has much to offer to the group when it comes time to discuss the book. It also helps me to learn about them; that Jon likes to raise his hand whether or not he has something to say or that Sarah needs to be lauded when on the rare occasion she does speak up.

STUDYING *CHARLOTTE'S WEB*

Once sufficient time has been devoted to personal responses to the book, I introduce the idea of annotation and close reading of a text. By annotating, I mean writing notes directly into the book and by close reading, I mean studying a text line by line. Doing this with a few pages of a book as carefully and beautifully written as *Charlotte's Web* can be an eye-opening experience for children. I show the class my own well-marked copy of *Charlotte's Web* as well as examples of published works such as *The Annotated Charlotte's Web*. I then explain to them that scholars do close readings of books and that we will be doing this with *Charlotte's Web*. While it is enjoyable to simply read a book for its story, it can also be interesting to dig deeper into a book and study what the author had in mind as he or she wrote it, how the author wrote it, and, perhaps, why.

A CLOSE READING OF CHAPTER 1

I demonstrate a close reading with Chapter 1. I show the children where I have underlined and made notes at certain places in the text. My initial close reading was done with Professor Ulrich Knoepflmacher during my NEH Summer Seminar at Princeton University, but subsequent readings alone and with children have caused me to add notes. Significant points in this first chapter are the references to death and the contrast between Fern's agitation and her mother and father's calm. White's wonderful descriptions are evident immediately, especially his description of a

breakfast of bacon. Thus White immediately makes clear the point of a pig on a farm: to produce bacon. Fern's brother Avery is also introduced, a contrast to the pacifistic Fern with his air rifle and wooden dagger. The chapter ends with Fern naming Wilbur. The connection to the author (White) with Wilbur (also "white") can be made.

To help focus on the life/death imagery, I create a chart and ask the children to look for words referring to life or death in the first chapter.

CHAPTER 1	
Life	**Death**
born	do away
springtime	die
love	kill
morning light	air rifle
breakfast	wooden dagger

We also investigate all the names to see if they have additional significance. For example, Arable means "plowable" and Fern is a plant. It is interesting to consider what White had in mind with names like Lurvy, Homer Zuckerman, Dr. Dorian, and Henry Fussy. (In the film, Henry is indeed a fussy child, but that does not come across in the book at all. His main role seems to be to draw Fern into adulthood and away from the barn.) It is fun to wonder how White selected names like Wilbur and Charlotte, solid "Americana" names.

Once we have completed Chapter 1, I have each child take a chapter to study. Since I usually have classes of twenty or twenty-one, this means one per child. If I had a larger class I would encourage children to double up on certain chapters. Again, we negotiate a deadline.

CHAPTER REPORTS

The reports on chapter studies take time. I tend to do them in two long class sessions, but other teachers who have used the unit prefer to conduct three or four shorter sessions. Each group will have its own temperament and need to be considered differently. It is a time-consuming, lengthy process, but most worthwhile. My role is to help the reporter along. Each child needs to feel like an expert on his/her chapter, yet it is also important not to lose the rest of the class if one child is going tediously through every line of the chapter. Sometimes, to speed things up, I ask them to report on one thing per page.

Children frequently note White's delightful descriptive passages. They note his love of smells and his frequent references to manure. They love his lists, especially the lists of Wilbur's meals. Often they note the change in point of view. At times the voice of the narrator (White) overrides that of the characters. They enjoy noting the shift in tone from reminiscences of summer days to the more direct dialogue of the barn animals.

One child, highly insecure about her reading ability, found a gem in the chapter where Charlotte dies. She noted that just as Charlotte dies alone in the midst of the fair, so she dies in the middle of the paragraph.

QUESTIONS TO PONDER

Over the years that I have taught this unit I have always asked the children to answer the following questions:

Who is the hero or heroine and why do you think so?

Who is selfish and why do you think so?

These two simple questions have provoked some of the most heated discussions regarding the book. Generally, the greatest disagreement is over considering Fern and/or Charlotte heroines. In the course of the discussion we start to define heroism. My students have tended to argue that heroism means saving a life. I have even had students argue that Templeton is a hero for bringing back the egg sac! For many, there is the feeling that Fern deserted Wilbur and thus lost her right to be heroic. Others feel she is still the heroine for saving Wilbur in the first place. The question always provokes and has never instigated a dull discussion. The question of selfishness is also one that animated the whole group. The children are just moving out of a self-involved childhood state themselves, so they are very sensitive to the idea of selfishness. While Wilbur would seem the most likely candidate for most selfish, Templeton is up there too, as is Homer Zuckerman.

THE WRITING OF CHARLOTTE'S WEB

The Annotated Charlotte's Web with Peter Neumeyer's notes and Scott Elledge's *E. B. White: A Biography* are excellent resources for exploring White's process in writing the book. Both have copies of pages in different drafts, White's notes on spiders, a drawing of the barn, etc. It is particularly interesting to examine the way White kept changing the beginning of the book. Fern did not exist in the earliest drafts; rather, the book began in the barn. It is fascinating to observe White revising and revising until later drafts begin to look like the beginning of the book we know today. Children are always deeply impressed with all the revising White did, and it invariably helps them to see the value of revision in their own work. If a great writer like E. B. White did so much, then they can too!

STUART LITTLE AND THE TRUMPET OF THE SWAN: SMALL GROUP STUDIES

I ask students to select either *Stuart Little* or *Trumpet of the Swan* for their second White book. I try to see to it that the groups are balanced in terms of numbers, but that is all. My experience has been that the children are truly interested in reading one or the other and do not make a decision based on one book being "easier" or because a friend will be in a particular group. I do not go into as detailed a study with these two books as I do with *Charlotte's Web*. The purpose here is to compare White's other books to *Charlotte's Web*.

The *Stuart Little* group often complains about the open-ended final chapter. They want Stuart to find Margalo. White intended it to be Stuart's journey into life, but my students don't always like this decision. Often, their frustration causes them to write new endings to the book that are more satisfactory to them.

One of the most interesting discussions about *The Trumpet of the Swan* concerned the way Louis negotiated Serena's freedom by offering one of their offspring to the zoo. My students were outraged that Louis did not consult Serena about the deal. They were horrified that Louis could give up a child so casually. Issues of adoption and foster care came up. The students were passionate and articulate.

During this part of the unit, I ask each child in the class to select a favorite passage from *Stuart Little* or *The Trumpet of the Swan* to prepare as a reading to the class. Every morning two or three children read to the class. The children greatly enjoyed this assignment. They took tremendous care with their choices and practiced well ahead of time. The others listened engrossed. We discovered some very fine readers in the class through this assignment and some very quiet children turned out to be dramatic readers.

E. B. WHITE PROJECTS: BRINGING IT ALL TOGETHER

The final part of the unit is the project section. The children work alone or in a group to prepare a project that brings out all their learning about E. B. White and his children's books. These projects are done as homework and presented on a day mutually agreed upon.

Some children have enjoyed performance projects. One year I had several video interviews of characters in all the books. Wilbur usually was played by a stuffed animal and several times Stuart was played by a pet gerbil. One year, a child created a video/puppet fantasy entitled "E. B. White in Paris." This child had White meeting characters from his books as he traveled around Paris. Yet another child spent hours on a claymation video involving characters from all three books.

CONCLUSION

An author study of E. B. White is an excellent way to start the school year. *Charlotte's Web*, *Stuart Little*, and *The Trumpet of the Swan* are children's classics in the true sense of the word: they are books children want to read again and again. These talking animals stories seem so real, no wonder my students create projects where Wilbur, Stuart, and Louise meet each other in story after story. Studying White and his writing of the books makes an impression on my young writers that they are not likely to forget.

Stuart and Wilbur

by Michael Benhabib

My name is Stuart Little. A few years ago I wrote a book about part of my life called *Stuart Little*, but I never finished it. I just published it and forgot about it. This was a big mistake because there's so much more to tell. So I decided to write the sequel to *Stuart Little*, *Stuart and Wilbur*.

It must have been about 2 or 3 hours after I drove out of Ames' Crossing when I came across a sign that read "Zuckerman's Famous Pig." There was an arrow pointing in the direction of a small dirt road. I was curious so I followed the arrow. The road was bumpy and there were trees on either side of it. This looked like the exact place I might find Margalo in. Margalo was my best friend. She was a red bird that disappeared from my parents' house in New York City. That was when I started my journey north to look for Margalo.

When I got to the end of the road I looked to the right of me and there was a house. Just a plain simple wooden house. To the left of me there was a barn. The barn was red and it wasn't very big and from the end of the road I could hear noises. All different kinds of noises. The noises of animals.

So I started to move closer and closer towards the barn until I was right next to the barn door. The door was open so I was just able to drive in. In the barn I saw all different kinds of animals: a pig, three spiders, a goose and some goslings, a lamb and there was a rat eating from the pig's trough. The animals in the barn stopped what they were doing and stared at me. The pig walked up to my car and said, "Hello, my name is Wilbur. Welcome to Zuckerman's barn."

"Hi, my name is Stuart Little. Have you seen a red bird lately?"

"No," said one of the spiders. "Why do you ask?" I told all the animals all about Margalo and why I was there.

Then one of the spiders said, "That's very sad."

"Yes, I know," I said. "By the way," I continued, "What is your name, please?"

"My name is Joy," said the spider. "And that's Aranea."

"I'm Nellie," said another one of the spiders.

(Stuart decides to stay at the barn in Templeton's nest.)

After a while I got very used to the barn and I thought I'd never leave. Actually, the barn was very nice, although Templeton seemed to have problems living with someone.

One afternoon I was talking to Wilbur about how much I liked this barn when I heard the sound of birds singing. I went outside and to my surprise I saw Margalo sitting on a tree and singing. I opened my mouth to speak but no words came out. Margalo stopped singing and flew down to me. Once Margalo had reached the ground she stammered, "S-S-S-Stuart? Is that you?"

"Y-Y-Yes," I stuttered.

"What are you doing here? How did you get here?" she said.

"Well," I answered, "I came looking for you."

(Margalo tells Stuart all her adventures and decides to move into Templeton's nest with Stuart.)

"SHE'S NOT STAYING IN MY NEST!" Templeton said in a loud voice.

"Oh, please let her stay!" begged Wilbur.

"Definitely not!" said Templeton.

"Oh, Templeton, you are nothing but a selfish rat!" said Wilbur in a loud voice.

"Fine, if you insist," said Templeton.

So Margalo stayed in Templeton's nest for many days. After a while she got very used to the barn and thought that she would never leave.

The barn was a very peaceful place. Year after year Margalo and I lived there and we are living there still.

STUDENT PACKET

E. B. WHITE:
An Author Study

INTRODUCTION

Charlotte's Web, *Stuart Little*, and *The Trumpet of the Swan* are three of the most well-known and best-loved books ever written for children. No doubt many of you are familiar with some or all of these books. You may have had *Stuart Little* read to you when you were little and watched the movie of *Charlotte's Web* more than once. Or you may have read all three books on your own. Those of you new to these books are in for a treat—they are truly wonderful pieces of literature.

For this first literature study we will be looking at the work of E. B. White. Not only will we read and discuss his children's books, but we will learn about White himself, his approach to writing, and how others have responded to his work.

BIOGRAPHICAL BACKGROUND

Elwyn Brooks White was born on July 11, 1899, in Mount Vernon, a suburb of New York City. His father was a piano manufacturer. His mother came from a musical family and also greatly loved nature, something she passed on to her son. White was an early avid reader and quickly became an accomplished writer, sending stories and poems to *St. Nicholas Magazine*, a popular journal for children. A great lover of outdoor activities, White suffered from terrible hay fever so his family decided to spend their summers in Maine where his hay fever wasn't so bad. White loved these summers and his fond memories show up in his writing, especially in *Stuart Little* and *The Trumpet of the Swan*.

White went to Cornell University and upon graduation began a career in journalism. After working at several newspapers and traveling throughout America, he moved to New York City and began writing for *The New Yorker*, then a new weekly magazine. Before long he took an editing job at the magazine and stayed associated with the magazine for the rest of his life. In 1929 he married Katherine Angell, a fellow editor at *The New Yorker*. Their son, Joel, was born a year later. Beginning in 1931, the Whites summered in Maine, eventually buying a farm and moving there in 1938. Six years later they moved back to New York, continuing to spend summers in Maine. Finally, in 1957, they moved back to Maine full-time. Whether in New York or Maine, White wrote. He was a great letter writer as well as a poet, essayist, and reporter. He died on October 1, 1985.

CHARLOTTE'S WEB

E. B. White spent a long time writing *Charlotte's Web*. He began work on a first draft in 1950, completing it on January 19, 1951. After numerous revisions the book was published to great acclaim on October 15, 1952. White did a tremendous amount of research for *Charlotte's Web*, watching life on the farm and learning all he could about spiders.

MEMORIES OF CHARLOTTE'S WEB

What do you know of *Charlotte's Web*? Was it read to you or do you know it in some other way? Please write your personal experiences with the story here. We will discuss these experiences with the whole class.

_____

_____

_____

_____

_____

_____

_____

READING
CHARLOTTE'S WEB

To begin we will all read *Charlotte's Web*. Each of you will have your own copy of the book. This way you can make the book your own. As we study the book, you may find parts that are special to you. Underline them, note them, write in the book and make it your personal *Charlotte's Web*. E. B. White wrote his *Charlotte's Web*, but everybody brings their own experiences to a reading of the book. Someone who has lived on a farm will read the book differently from someone who has only lived in a city. This means that my *Charlotte's Web* will be different from yours.

Remember, everyone in this class is part of our reading community. This means that we will decide together how much time *everyone* in the class needs to comfortably read the book. Fast readers are not necessarily good readers. In a community of readers, everyone is respected as a reader. Those who take their time reading a book are as important in our reading community as those who will finish a book in a day. If you finish *Charlotte's Web* before others, you should continue reading your independent book. Realize that even if you have read this book ten times already, you will need to read it again for this assignment. Scholars reread books many times to better understand them. I reread *Charlotte's Web* every year, and learn something more about it every time I read it. If you reread it with the idea that you are reading it in a new way and hoping to learn something new, it will be an enjoyable experience for you. That is what being a literary scholar is all about.

READING PLAN FOR *CHARLOTTE'S WEB*

Work out a schedule for completing the book on the agreed-upon date.

Week   Chapters

_____

_____

_____

_____

_____

Due date: _____

RESPONDING TO *CHARLOTTE'S WEB*

We will not discuss *Charlotte's Web* as a whole class until everyone has finished reading it. However, you are welcome to discuss it with your classmates, with me, and with your family. If you are bursting to talk about an event in the book, please do so! Just do so quietly so that others can read. If you are at home, by all means read a favorite section aloud to your little sister or brother, or even to your mother! Use your journals for written responses. I love to read your entries and write back to you.

STUDYING
CHARLOTTE'S WEB

Once everyone has finished the book we will discuss it as a whole class. First we will just discuss what we enjoyed about the book, what we noticed, what struck us most. Then we will look more closely at the book as literary scholars. I will present some of the methods scholars use when studying an author and particular books. Specifically, you will learn how to annotate your copy of *Charlotte's Web*. This means underlining lines in the book that seem important to you and writing notes about the book in the margins. We will do a close reading of the first chapter all together and then each of you will do a close study of one chapter and present your findings to the class.

During our work with *Charlotte's Web*, we will listen to a tape of White reading *Charlotte's Web* and learn more about him as a writer. As we learn about the way he wrote *Charlotte's Web*, we will be learning more about what it means to be a writer.

QUESTIONS TO PONDER
AND ARGUE ABOUT
CHARLOTTE'S WEB

Every year many questions come up during our discussions. The two that follow are great for getting started. Please answer them thoughtfully in preparation for our class discussion.

Who do you think is the hero or heroine? Why?

_____

_____

_____

_____

_____

Who do you think is selfish? Why?

_____

_____

_____

_____

_____

_____

_____

STUART LITTLE

White's first children's book was *Stuart Little*. He had been telling Stuart stories to nieces, nephews, and his son for years before he decided to write them down. He began writing it in 1939 and then put it away until 1944 when he finished it. *Stuart Little* came out in October 1945. It was a huge success, eventually translated into twenty languages.

THE TRUMPET OF THE SWAN

The Trumpet of the Swan was White's last children's book. He used memories of his childhood camp in Maine as well as the careful research he always did for his books. His manuscript for the book was completed in 1969, and White sent it right to his editor rather than putting it away for awhile as he had done with his other books. An immediate success like his other children's books, *Trumpet of the Swan* quickly became a best-seller. Today, it is less known than *Charlotte's Web* and *Stuart Little*, but still widely read.

STUART LITTLE AND
THE TRUMPET OF THE SWAN
STUDY GROUPS

You will select either *Stuart Little* or *The Trumpet of the Swan* for this part of the unit and read, discuss, and study it with others in the class who are reading the same book. You are welcome to read all three books, but I would like you to spend some time in a smaller group studying one book in depth. Finally, the whole class will come together for a discussion on all of the books, how they connect, and some final thoughts on White and his books.

What connections can you see between *Charlotte's Web* and the book you read (*Stuart Little/Trumpet of the Swan*)?

_____

_____

_____

_____

_____

_____

_____

_____

FINAL E. B. WHITE
PROJECTS

As a final response to this unit, you will create a project that will combine all you have felt and learned from reading and studying White's children's books.

Here are some ideas, but you are welcome to come up with your own:

- ❀ Create a piece of art combining characters and scenes from the different books.

- ❀ Create a map of one of the books.

- ❀ Create an original comic book using characters from the different books.

- ❀ Create a skit or play using characters and ideas from the books.

- ❀ Create a story about E. B. White and characters from his books.

- ❀ Write a sequel to one of the books.

- ❀ Create a puppet show with characters from the books.

- ❀ Write an original story inspired by the books.

- ❀ Create a video around the books.

- ❀ Create a poem inspired by the books.

- ❀ Come up with your own idea.

PROJECT PLAN

Please write a description of your project and a plan for completing it in a timely fashion.

_____

_____

_____

_____

_____

_____

Project due: _____

CHAPTER 4

A Thematic Study of Cinderella

*"It's like being Cinderella. You wear your suit
and go there and you have to be back in the projects
by midnight."*

JAMEL OESER-SWEAT, WESTINGHOUSE SCIENCE
TALENT SEARCH TALENT SEARCH FINALIST
NEW YORK TIMES, JANUARY 30, 1994

airy tales are fantasy stories that everyone knows. References to fairy tales abound in our lives. We use them without thinking: "What a witch!" "If the shoe fits." "The wolf is at the door." A thematic study of one well-known fairy tale can provide children with a deeper understanding of traditional literature as well as an opportunity to explore the myriad ways the tale has become part of our culture. *Cinderella* is particularly suitable for such a study because it seems so universal. The theme we associate with *Cinderella* is "rags to riches," a compelling one that manifests itself over and over again in tales, literature, and images all over the world. It is recognizable in the ad for a new, improved detergent that makes clothes clean (ashes to ball gown) as well as in the poor boy who becomes a great President (Abraham Lincoln.) The study can go in numerous directions depending on the interest of the teacher and students. Opportunities exist for exploring the tale in other cultures, in parodies, in comparison to other tales, in popular culture, in history, and in literature. It is a unit rich with possibilities.

CINDERELLA BACKGROUND

SOME HISTORY

Versions of the *Cinderella* story have been around in one form or another for hundreds of years. The ninth-century Chinese manuscript of *Yeh Shen* is thought to be the oldest written version of the tale. Charles Perrault truly popularized the tale in Europe by including it in his 1697 fairy tale collection, *Tales of My Mother Goose*. It is the Perrault version, complete with fairy godmother, pumpkin, and glass slippers, that has become the definitive *Cinderella* for Americans today, mostly due to Disney's 1949 animated film. However, less well-known versions exist from many different parts of the world. The German Grimm Brothers published their version (sans godmother) in their nineteenth-century collection of fairy tales. While the version we knows seems distinctly European, folklorists are constantly discovering non-Western variants of the tale. Modern writers have also taken to the tale, often parodying it or utilizing the rags-to-riches theme for their own purposes.

CINDERELLA TALE TYPES

Folklorists use the term "tale type" to refer to a particular story line. Marian Roalfe Cox noted five types in *Cinderella, Three Hundred and Forty-Five Variants of Cinderella, Catskin, and Cap o'Rushes, Abstracted and Tabulated* (1893). Aarne and Thompson identified three types in *The Types of the Folktale* (1961). Both note significant elements such as the persecuted heroine, magical help, the ball, and the slipper test. Neil Philip, in *The Cinderella Story* (1988), writes "There are numerous ways of categorizing the Cinderella variants, depending on the nature and the order of the incidents. Many areas have distinctive traditions. But it is essentially true to say that there are two main strands of story: one in which the girl is mistreated and humiliated because of her stepmother's jealousy, and one in which her suffering is caused by her father's incestuous desires." (p. 3) Teachers seriously committed to this unit need to be aware of both strands since the former is the only one which tends to be found in children's books, though there are occasionally veiled allusions to the latter. Perrault's *Cinderella* typifies the former strand while Charlotte Huck's *Princess Furball* (1989) is a sanitized version of the latter.

CINDERELLA IN THE CLASSROOM

THE *CINDERELLA* CENTER

I have a classroom divided into work areas, meeting areas, and a cozy reading area, carpeted and full of pillows with a classroom library located nearby. For each new literary study I set up a learning center in my reading area. Sometimes there are only a few books and students add their own work to the center as the unit gets underway. In the case of the *Cinderella* Study, I create a full-fledged learning center, designed to excite and intrigue my students. Picture books and fairy tale collections are invitingly displayed as well as cartoons, ads, newspaper headlines, and other *Cinderella* references. It is easy to build a collection for this unit. Publishers are constantly coming out with inexpensive new versions of this old tale as well as fairy tale collections. School and public libraries are generally well stocked with fairy tales. You will be amazed how often you will see references to *Cinderella* once you begin such a unit. Keep an eye out for references in advertisements and in magazine and newspaper headlines.

Encourage your students to add to the Center. As we got deeper into our study and our definition of what a *Cinderella* tale is broadened, my students relished the search for the nonconventional *Cinderella*— Charles Dickens's *Oliver Twist* or a tale of a baseball rookie who made it big. Parents and others in the school community should also be encouraged to contribute.

GETTING STARTED

I begin the *Cinderella* Study by reading a silly *Cinderella* variant such as Roald Dahl's in *Revolting Rhymes* (1998) or Babette Cole's *Prince Cinders* (1987) to whet my students' appetites for the fun ahead. I then give each child a packet which includes an introduction to the unit, activities, charts, and a bibliography.

PERSONAL FAIRY TALE DEFINITIONS

The first activity asks the children to write their own definitions of the term "fairy tale." The children are encouraged to write whatever they wish. I inform them that there is no such thing as one "right" definition for "fairy tale." My students' initial definitions have included fairy tales as "fantasy or illusion," full of "dragons and wizards," and "a fiction book that is the kind of book that a mother can read to her four-year-old son or daughter."

MEMORIES OF *CINDERELLA*

Next I have the children retell *Cinderella*. For this activity we sit in a circle. Children either volunteer to add to the evolving story, or I simply have them tell parts of the story as we go around the circle. Of course, it quickly becomes clear where their memories of *Cinderella* come from—the Disney movie, of course! Sometimes, children will have vague recollections of someone reading the story to them, but for the vast majority it is Disney's version (and especially those mice) that stays in their memories!

ANALYSES OF SOME *CINDERELLA* VARIANTS

We now move into the heart of the unit. Students are asked to investigate a wide variety of *Cinderella* variants and keep track of their research in charts provided as part of their packets. The charts are structured to encourage students to expand their idea of what a *Cinderella* story is. The information is intentionally kept to a minimum so that filling out the charts isn't a chore or simply a mindless task. The children quickly learn what a genre is and enjoy distinguishing picture books from videos from poems and chapter books in their explorations. I have found that the culture category occasionally gives them trouble. There is no problem with obvious variants like Shirley Climo's *The Korean Cinderella* (1989). Difficulties come up with more subtle distinctions like American versus Canadian or American versions of Perrault's French story. However, such dilemmas also reinforce the idea that fairy tales can't be simplified and labeled in any one way. Finally, the personal response section gives children a quick and easy way to give their own opinions about the versions they are studying. I ask for deeper, more insightful responses in their journals.

Children explore *Cinderella* variants in many ways: individual or paired readings, read alouds, and videos. To begin their explorations of *Cinderella*, I require that all children in the class be exposed to a number of variants. This gives us all a frame of reference for discussion. Some of these required texts are read by the children independently or in pairs, others I read aloud to the class. The children then move on to choose among the many texts available to them.

I set aside a *Cinderella* Time every day. It

is structured to be quite predictable: I begin with a group experience, perhaps reading a *Cinderella* to the whole group or leading a discussion on a text all have read. At this time I allow discussion of other media versions of *Cinderella*, for example a television show or ad. After the whole-group time there is some workshop time which the children use to read alone or with a friend and to work on filling in their charts.

TEXTS

RECOMMENDED STUDENT READINGS

Perrault, Charles. (1969). "Cinderella or The Little Glass Slipper." Trans. by A. E. Johnson. In *Perrault's Fairy Tales*. New York: Dover.

This is an early English translation of Perrault's tale. I feel it is very important for the children to read the original Perrault. This version is easy for children to read. Many early editions have small type and archaic conventions (such as no quotation marks in dialogues). Given the difficulty of the vocabulary I felt I could not also expect children to struggle through a text formatted in an unfamiliar way. I used to retyped the tale to make it more accessible, but later came across this edition which is excellent for children. The print is large and the style is familiar. I ask my students to read this text on their own. Some will read it aloud with partners, others silently alone. Since they are already familiar with the plot the vocabulary does not seem to be a problem for them. I considered creating a glossary for them, but found it was unnecessary. They seemed comfortable using context clues to help them with unfamiliar words.

Brothers Grimm. (1987). "Cinderella." In *The Complete Fairy Tales of the Brothers Grimm*. Trans. by Jack Zipes. New York: Bantam.

After Perrault, the Grimm fairy tales are most well known to us. However, we tend to be less familiar with the Grimm version of *Cinderella*. My students are invariably surprised by the lack of a godmother and the harshness of certain elements of the text such as the cutting off of the stepsisters' toe and heel and the pecking out of their eyes at the end. Certainly adults have been uncomfortable with this imagery in the past with the result that the Perrault version, which has no blood, has dominated. Much has been written about the Grimm tales and their effect on children. Today, with all the violence of video games, television shows, and films such as *Home Alone*, the Grimm tales seem mild.

There are many versions of the Grimm tales available. This one is well translated, and my students have had no difficulty reading it independently despite its small print.

Chase, Richard. (1976). "Ashpet." In *Grandfather Tales*. Boston: Houghton Mifflin.

My children read this Appalachian variant on their own. It is clearly based on the well-known European versions, yet the landscape and language are those of the American Appalachian people. It would also work well as a read aloud or even in a storytelling situation. Later in the unit the children are able to contrast this version with Tom Davenport's film, a very different *Ashpet*.

Steptoe, John. (1987). *Mufaro's Beautiful Daughters*. New York: Lothrop, Lee & Shepard.

This is a beautiful book. Children can savor it on their own, in pairs, or in a group reading using the big book version. Steptoe was inspired by a visit to Zimbabwe and a story he found in a nineteenth-century collection of South African folktales. It is a different telling of the *Cinderella* story in a totally different environment. It is an excellent transition into versions that don't have balls, pumpkins, and shoe tests.

Louie, Ai-Ling. *Yeh-Shen.* (1982). Illustrated by Ed Young. New York: Philomel.

Wilson, Barbara Ker. *Wishbones.* (1993). Illustrated by Meilo So. New York: Bradbury.

Two beautiful non-Western tellings of the oldest Cinderella story. The Louie book has a copy of the Chinese text in the front. Before I had the Wilson book, I used only Louie's book. During one of my class discussions of the tale, a Chinese teacher was visiting. She told us that Louie had not completed the tale, ending it with the marriage when it actually went on beyond that. Wilson's book continue the story to its ancient conclusion. It is interesting that Louie chose to end the story prematurely at the point where Westerners are most comfortable, while Wilson was more true to the original text. This makes for an interesting discussion.

By the way, our Chinese visitor was fascinated that we would even consider Yeh-Shen a Cinderella. She told us the Chinese consider *Cinderella* to be the European tale alone.

TEACHER READ ALOUDS

Viorst, Judith. ". . .And Then the Prince Knelt Down and Tried to Put the Glass Slipper on Cinderella's Foot." (1987). In *Don't Bet on The Prince: Contemporary Feminist Fairy Tales in North America and England.* New York: Routledge.

This is an extremely brief, witty poem. I read it to the children at the beginning of our study.

Dahl, Roald. "Cinderella." (1988). In *Revolting Rhymes.* Illustrated by Quentin Blake. New York: Bantam.

The book's title says it all. Dahl relishes turning everything in the tale around in a sing-song verse. I use this early on to illustrate how well-known authors parody the tale.

Cole, Babette. (1987). *Prince Cinders.* New York: Sandcastle Books.

Here we have a gender switch done with wit and humor. It is a good way to introduce the idea that Cinderella does not have to be a girl.

Yorink, Arthur. (1990). *Ugh.* Illustrated by Richard Egielski. New York: Farrar Straus Giroux.

I admit to tremendous fondness for this picture book. It is another male Cinderella situated in an ersatz Stone Age. The plot line, text, and illustrations are very clever, especially the twist on the slipper test.

Lardner, Ring. (1926). "Cinderella." In *What Of It?* New York: Scribner's.

This is a delightful twenties parody of the classic tale. Lardner has a free hand with the vernacular and activities of the period (think *Guys and Dolls*). Cinderella is Zelda and the Prince is named Scott (Fitzgerald, perhaps?).

Sexton, Anne. (1971). "Cinderella." In *Transformations.* Boston: Houghton Mifflin.

I read this to my class. It is an adult poem, but the feeling of disappointment is something that I feel children can understand. In the real world, fairy tales don't always happen. This poem is a sardonic looking back by a Cinderella who found it wasn't quite "happily ever after."

VIDEO *CINDERELLAS*

There are movies galore about Cinderella. The rags-to-riches theme seems remarkably prevalent in Hollywood movies. Every year there seem to be a few out, often related to sports. My students adore exploring this theme in film. I usually show all or parts of several films and then lead discussions contrasting and comparing the films to each other as well as to printed materials. In the bibliography are a number of Cinderella and Cinderella-themed movies. I have found the following videos to work with great success:

Rossini's La Cenerentola.
This is a version filmed at La Scala in Milan. Evidently there was already a Cinderella opera out at the time that Rossini began this one so there is no shoe test; rather, bracelets are featured. I like exposing my students to a different medium such as opera, and this particular version is so well done that they quite enjoy the parts I show.

Jerry Lewis's Cinderfella.
The children love this one! It takes place in 1960's Beverly Hills with Ed Wynn as a rather rotund fairy godfather. A patent leather evening shoe is featured during the ball.

Tom Davenport's Ashpet.
This is a delightful version of the Appalachian story, different from Chase's version. An African-American storyteller is Aunt Sally, the fairy godmother of this version.

Usually when I'm leading a discussion comparing versions I like to make a chart. The chart on the following page I made as we compared the three videos. The children decided on the categories.

THE *CINDERELLA* THEME IN POPULAR CULTURE AND ELSEWHERE

I encourage my students to look beyond the usual places to find the rags-to-riches theme. Many enjoy looking on the sports pages. For example, the stunning upset of the semifinals for the 1994 World Cup involved underdog Bulgaria defeating the expected winner Germany. The *New York Times* headline of July 11, 1994, was: "Bulgaria, a Small Foot in Soccer, Steps Closer to Glass Slipper." Another child was able to convince me that Disney's *Aladdin* was a Cinderella story, very much a rags-to-riches tale. Chapter books such as Burnett's *The Little Princess* are often mentioned.

STUDENT RESPONSES TO *CINDERELLAS*

Response journals are part of the fabric of my classroom. Thus, the children are comfortable when asked to write a more extended response to a particular video or books.

Lexy's response to *Cinderfella*:

I thought it was very funny and nice. It was very different than most Cinderellas. For instance in this one Fella was pretty dumb and not too handsome. But Cinderella is always very pretty.

53

COMPARING VIDEO CINDIES

Categories	La Cenerentola	Cinderfella	Ashpet
Family	Mean stepfather silly stepsisters: mean and greedy	Stepmother and stepbrothers mean, just want money. (stepmother feels sorry at end)	Stepmother: nice stepsisters: mean
Magical helper	Aliadoro prince's tutor	Fairy godfather	Aunt Sally
Where they lived	house in countryside	LA mansion	Farmhouse
Ball	Ball	Ball	Goodbye dance for soldiers
Test object	Bracelets	Patent leather dress shoe	Glass shoe
Test	Valet/Prince Switch (Cinderella falls for valet who is really the prince)	People/Person (Jerry is People Princess is Person)	Niceness Riddles True Love
Culture	Italian	Californian	Appalachian
Time	1800's	1960's	World War II
Animals	none	fish	horse

I liked the fairy godfather. He was really funny. Especially with his wise cracks. I think Charlie Chaplin would make a good Fella because Chaplin is just perfect for the role.

My response to Lexy:

Dear Lexy,

I am intrigued by your idea of Chaplin as Fella. Actually, don't you think some of his films are Cinderella stories? (I'd shown a number of Chaplin shorts and features to my class.) His Little Tramp character is certainly a Cinderella-like person, don't you think? Check out Modern Times—see if that is a Cinderella story.

Eric on his favorite variant:

I liked the Grimm Brothers Cinderella because sometimes I think that other Cinderellas are too babyish (At least at my age that's what I think.) For example, when the birds poke the stepsister's eyes out. I don't think any mom would tell their 3 year old son that.

Eric on the *Cinderella* theme in an independent reading book:

I am reading a book called *Charlie and the Chocolate Factory.* It is very good. I like it because Charlie (a boy who loves chocolate) who lives in a very poor family, all of a sudden becomes the owner of Mr. Wonka's giant chocolate factory. I think it is kind of a *Cinderella* story. The "ball" is the tour of the chocolate factory. Then when Charlie becomes the owner of the chocolate factory, that is kind of like Cinderella with the prince except the "palace" is the chocolate factory.

Comparing *Cinderella* to Another Fairy Tale

After my students have spent some time on *Cinderella,* I ask them to select another fairy tale as a comparison. Then they become storytellers, practicing the tale and telling it to their classmates just as the tales were originally told. I then ask them to write how their favorite *Cinderella* variant is similar to and different from this tale.

Redefining Fairy Tale

After several weeks of research, discussion, and analysis, I ask my students to consider their definition of *fairy tale* and to write a new definition based on their work. We have a class discussion about these definitions, whether they have changed, and if so why. Then we attempt to create a class definition of fairy tales. The following chart was created during one such

discussion. It is full of phrases taken from students, by no means a polished final definition of *fairy tale.*

One Class's Ideas About Fairy Tales

Often, but not always, something magic
A short story
A lot of them have tests
Predictable beginnings and endings
Unlikely to *really* happen
Make-believe
Often have magical helpers
Sometimes scary
Usually starts off not too good and ends up good for main character
Often going somewhere
Nice inside/bad-looking outside
Teaches bad guys a lesson and reader/listener
Has a moral
Significance of parents
Teaches kids what is wrong or right

CINDERELLA PROJECT

CINDERELLA MOTIFS

In preparation for writing their own variants, I have a group discussion itemizing what makes a *Cinderella* story. I note the children's comments on large chart paper. One year my class came up with the following:

One Class's List of *Cinderella* Motifs

There is a test.
Some kind of class distinction often involving royalty.
There is a big event: "the ball."
Have predictable beginnings and endings ("Once upon a

time...happily ever after.")
Dead mother.
Step-parents and step-siblings.
Someone mean.
Wedding/marriage/fame/wealth.
Proves a point/often a moral.
Gets something good at the end.
Threes.
Animals (fish, birds, mice, lizards,
    horses, dinosaurs, dogs, cats,
    oxen...)
Lost objects (shoes, bracelets, ring,
    necklace, earrings, bike, trousers,
    sneakers...)
Helper (fairy godmother or
    godfather, trees, eggs, fishbones,
    birds, dead mother)

CHILDREN'S VARIANTS

Now the children create their own *Cinderella* variants. I have found that most children want to write their own versions. Since I encourage video, illustrative, and performance projects during other units, I have emphasized works on paper for this one. In fact, the assignment is for each student to create an original *Cinderella* to contribute to a class *Cindy* book.

It has been fascinating to observe the different directions the children have gone. Many stay with the familiar strand, complete with fairy godmother figure and test. Sometimes, students choose to take less-known paths and create stories involving tests of character. One year I had a class of children who were television addicts. I gave them an open invitation to use characters from their favorite shows in their stories. The result were "Saved by the Bell" and "Beverly Hills 90210" variants. The latter inspired one child to write of Brenda wanting to go to a beach party but not having a bikini to wear. Fortunately it is provided by a fairy godmother. The final test object is Brenda's hair ornament. Another story involved sibling rivalry

between Bart and Lisa Simpson. Still another involved a rich stepmother who shopped all day. The Cinderella character used the stepmother's American Express card to get her clothes for the disco.

The excerpts beginning on page 57 are from my students' stories.

THE *CINDY* CELEBRATION

Children need an opportunity to present their work to an audience. A great way to do this is with a reading. After putting together our *Cindy* book, we invited parents and friends to a *Cindy* Celebration. Refreshments included an enormous rice krispy treat in the shape of a slipper and slipper cookies. Charts, books, art, and the like were displayed throughout the room. Each child made a brief presentation of their choice. Most wanted to read excerpts from their stories. Some chose to read a favorite variant by someone else. One student had written a lengthy play called "The Three Princesses." She and her friends had a wonderful time performing part of it before the assembled guests. A grand time was had by all!

Baseballella

by Matthew Spiro

Once upon a time there was a baseball team called the Hoppin Jalapenos. They were an expansion team, they were considered the worst team in the league, expected to go 0-15, pretty bad huh! All the other teams teased them, especially the defending champs, the High Hawks. . . .

It was the day of the championship. The whole team was in the locker room. All of a sudden they heard a click. They were locked in! There were ten minutes left till game time, they were still locked in! All of a sudden there was a flash! Five seconds later standing right in front of them was Mickey Mantle! Not one could believe their eyes. Then Mickey said, "Do you want to go and play?"

"Yes," the team said. Just like that Mickey swung his golden bat and ... the whole team had new uniforms, new cleats, and golden gloves.

Then Mickey said, "Be back in the locker room right after the game because everything will disappear." With one minute left till game time, Mickey swung his bat and knocked the door down. The Jalapenos took the field just in time. . . .

They won the championship!! They were definitely the best expansion team ever in the league. With no time to celebrate, they dropped their mitts, and ran into the locker room.

One week later it was time for the trophy ceremony. Everyone was excited. Since the champs had fled from the scene, a lot of people were claiming to be on the Jalapenos so they could get the trophy. The league officials couldn't find the list of the teams, and who was on them. Since the champs had left their gloves on the diamond, the league officials had every person in the league (they did have the league register) try on the gloves.

Once they had the Jalapenos all together, they gave them the trophy. Even though the Hawks teased them they still gave them a second place banner.

They have never lost a game since then!

Cinderella Goes to CAMP!

by Erica Bromley

There once was a little girl who lived with her father in a town in New Jersey. The girl's name was Ella and she was 7. She loved her father very much but her father was very sick. Her father died when he was 47, when Ella had just turned 8. Ell went to live with her aunt and cousins in New York. Ell's cousin's names were Elizabeth and Rose. They were twins, they were nice to her when her father was around but they were mean to her now.

When Ella was 9 her aunt sent Ella and her cousins to sleepaway camp for the summer. Ella was in Elizabeth and Rose's bunk and she was really disappointed. . . .

Finally it was Saturday the day it was night swim. Ella's cousins got into their bathing suits and got ready to go down to the lake. When everyone was ready to go Ella's cousins locked her in the SMELLY bathroom, but when they were walking to swim Ella's counselors asked Elizabeth and Rose where Ella was. They said, "I don't know." but really they did. . . .

So 12 years later Ella and Charlie got married and became directors of the camp. And they all lived happily ever after, except for the cousins. Who knows what happened to them!!

Shoerella

by Anna Monaco

Once upon a time there was a shoe named Ella. She was a very kind-hearted shoe and she was very energetic. When Ella was very young her mother died from athlete's foot and after that she was very very sad. So her father went to war for a year, then came back and married a female shoe named Tabitha. Tabitha had two ugly, annoying, selfish, conceited, well I could go on and on about them, but why don't we just get on with the story. . . .

After they left (for the ball) Ella went to the kitchen to get something to eat when all of a sudden there was a big crash and the sound of glass breaking. When Ella opened her eyes she saw a glass shoe. "Darn, I broke my heel."

"Who are you?"

"I am your father's mother's cousin's brother's fairy glass slipper."

Ovenella or the Little Brass Knuckles

by Steven Rosenblatt

   Once upon a time there was a girl named Ovenella.
She was a rough and tough girl. They called her
Ovenella because she was always around the oven, but
it is not like she wanted to be around the oven. She
was always around the oven because her mean uncle,
Kicky the kick boxer, would kick her if he saw her any
place else. . . .

   So then the gang leader went there and asked
Ovenella to try on the brass knuckles and when she did
they were a perfect fit and then magically her gang
clothes came back and she ran away with Rocky (the
gang leader) and they lived happily ever after.

Cinderella Poem

by Anne Kurtz

Come and enjoy your stay with us on our adventure to the palace and let's find out about how Cinderella is doing. Cinderella has been enjoying herself a lot more than she has in the past.

In the palace is a very active place. But even though they are very busy they still hold balls and Cinderella invites her step sisters and stepmother.

Never in Cinderella's life did she think that she would marry the prince. Even though she did want to marry the prince a little bit.

Decisions are very important in the palace for instance a cress, what to drink, what to eat, what to do.

Every person in the town can attend Cinderella's balls.

Really it's not so bad even though sometimes she misses her old family.

Every time Cinderella wants something she gets it but now that that has happened a lot she doesn't like to be treated like that.

Let's look around the house. Cinderella has some of the most expensive things around.

Lots of things are different from the way she used to live. So when she gets homesick she just cries.

Any time you go to Cinderella's house you are welcome because she loves visitors.

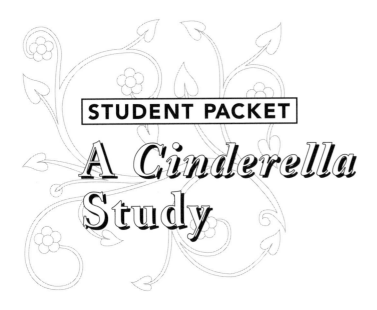

STUDENT PACKET

A Cinderella Study

"Once upon a time. . . Happily ever after." These words usually surround the stories we know as fairy tales. For there is no doubt in our minds when we read the words "Once upon a time" that a certain kind of story will follow: a fairy tale. Why is this? What is a fairy tale exactly? Is it different from other kinds of stories? Where do fairy tales come from? Why are they called fairy tales anyway?

To help us define what a fairy tale is we are going to take a close look at one well-known tale, *Cinderella*. It seems like everyone knows that story. "Rags to riches" is a popular theme in movies, books, and television shows. Dreaming of winning the lottery, becoming a movie star, making millions in the stock market are all Cinderella dreams, aren't they? We love to watch a Cinderella team move from the bottom of a league to win the pennant or to watch someone go from childhood poverty to become a multimillionaire music star. I think we all want to be Cinderellas!

While it may seem like *Cinderella* belongs to America, it actually comes from far away. In fact, the oldest Cinderella stories come from Asia and scholars have found hundreds of *Cinderella* tales all over the world. We will be studying some of these variants as well as other offshoots of the tale. There will be picture book Cinderellas, video Cinderellas, movie Cinderellas, rap Cinderellas, poetry Cinderellas, male and female Cinderellas, American Cinderellas, African Cinderellas, German Cinderellas, funny Cinderellas, sad Cinderellas, television Cinderellas, operatic Cinderellas, silly Cinderellas, and many many more!

So let's get started! May the shoe fit!

1. Personal fairy tale definitions.

Please write your definition of a fairy tale. Don't worry about trying to come up with the one "right" definition because there isn't one! Just write down your personal idea of a fairy tale.

_____

_____

_____

_____

_____

_____

2. Memories of *Cinderella*.

What is your version of *Cinderella*? We will do a retelling of the tale with everyone in the class contributing elements from their own personal version. Then we will discuss how each of us got these versions in our heads. Did your grandmother first tell you the tale? Did you read it in a book? Perhaps you got your idea from a movie. Let's find out.

_____

_____

_____

_____

_____

_____

_____

3. Analyses of some *Cinderella* variants.

You will be looking at many many different versions. I will also be reading versions to you. To keep track of all the variants please use the charts that I will give you. They will serve as a record of all the different *Cinderellas* you study and help you as you begin to create a description of what a *Cinderella* story really is.

4. Now become a storyteller. Before fairy tales were written down, people told them to each other. Chose a non-Cinderella fairy tale. Learn it and practice telling it. We will tell our fairy tales to each other.

5. Now select a favorite *Cinderella* and compare it to the fairy tale you told.

Cinderella _____

Fairy Tale _____

How are they alike?

_____

_____

_____

_____

_____

_____

How are they different?

_____

_____

_____

_____

_____

_____

6. Without looking back at your first definition write your current definition of fairy tale.

_____

_____

_____

_____

_____

_____

When you are done (not before, please!) take a look at your first definition. We will have a class discussion on whether our ideas of fairy tales have changed from this study and if they have, why.

7. Now that we have studied many many different *Cinderella* variants it is time for us to come up with the elements or motifs that make up a *Cinderella* story. Clearly all the versions we have been studying have things in common. What are some of those things?

_____

_____

_____

_____

_____

_____

_____

8. Now it is your turn! You will create your own *Cinderella* variant! Select your own genre and style. Your work will be published in a class *Cinderella* Book which will be presented at a *Cindy* Celebration!

CINDERELLA VARIANTS THAT I HAVE STUDIED

Title	Author Illustrator	Genre (e.g. picture book, movie, T.V. show, song, poem, etc.)	Culture (e.g. Chinese, French, German, etc.)	Personal Response (What did you think of it?)

VISUALIZING FANTASY: A Study of *Alice in Wonderland* and Its Illustrators

...once or twice she had peeped into the book her sister was reading, but it had no pictures or conversations in it, "and what is the use of a book," thought Alice, "without pictures or conversations?"

LEWIS CARROLL, *ALICE IN WONDERLAND*

lice in Wonderland was my favorite book as a child. My father read it to me, and later I read it again and again on my own. The wildness of characters like the Cheshire Cat and the Mock Turtle, the witty word play, the complete and utterly fantastic nature of Wonderland drew me in time and again. Tenniel's illustrations had much to do with my adoration; his Alice was my Alice and I couldn't imagine the characters any other way.

My first exposure to other artists' illustrations of *Alice in Wonderland* was at the British Library in London, where I saw Lewis Carroll's original manuscript for the story, *Alice's Adventures Underground*. He did his own illustrations, and they were nothing like Tenniel's. Carroll's Alice was a dark haired pre-Raphaelite, a direct contrast to Tenniel's little blond in a pinafore. During my NEH seminar at Princeton in 1990, I did research on the illustrators of Alice in Wonderland. To my delight, I found a myriad of wonderful illustrators of the book. It turned out that illustrating *Alice in Wonderland* was the pinnacle of many an artist's career. Many well-known illustrators have attempted Carroll's book; it seems to be like *Hamlet* is for actors—all the greats attempt it. Studying the many different ways illustrators have approached *Alice in Wonderland* makes for a fascinating literature unit.

Is *Alice in Wonderland* for Children?

There are many adults today who will insist that *Alice in Wonderland* is too sophisticated, too strange, and too scary for children. But it is important to remember that Lewis Carroll told the original story to a little girl and wrote it for children. He wanted to write a different kind of children's book, one with a cranky, imperfect heroine, without a moral, with wit and humor. Indeed, Wonderland is a very strange place. Carroll meant it to be a dream, and to include all the weirdness of a dream. Yet peculiar as the characters may be, none is actually frightening in the manner of a horror book. The most threatening character may be the Queen, and Alice doesn't seem particularly concerned about her. Rather, one of the amusing aspects of the book is the way Alice, a little girl, often appears larger and more frightening to the characters than they are to her. While *Alice in Wonderland* can be and has been studied by adult scholars, it is first of all a children's book. It has been enjoyed by numerous children, all over the world, for over a century.

Lewis Carroll

ewis Carroll was a rather eccentric Englishman, a mathematics instructor and clergyman at Christ Church College in Oxford. He was born in 1832 as Charles Lutwidge Dodgson, the eldest of eleven children. Even as a child his talent was evident as he clearly enjoyed entertaining his younger siblings with stories and games. As an adult he became an amateur photographer as well as a writer of mathematical books. A shy man due to a stammer, he never married although he developed close attachments to a number of young girls over the years. While this may give us pause today, his affections were not untypical for Victorians. There is not a shred of evidence that his interactions with children were anything but completely appropriate.

While Carroll had many child friends in the course of his life, one of his favorites was certainly Alice Liddell, the little girl to whom he first told the Alice stories. He first told the story on a lazy rowboat outing on a warm summer afternoon. Eventually he wrote the story down and showed it to some friends who encouraged him to publish it. He did so, and the book was a raging success. It prompted him to do a nursery version, to oversee theatrical versions, to produce toys related to the book (Disney did not invent the tie-in), and finally to write a sequel, *Alice Through the Looking-glass.*

Carroll wrote several other children's books; however, none was as successful as the two *Alice* books. He died in1898.

The *Alice* Center

efore beginning this unit I set up an *Alice* Center in my classroom. It consists of many different illustrated editions of *Alice in Wonderland* as well as other material related to the story, the author, and the period. I constantly come across cartoons, headlines, and ads that refer to Alice. I keep these and display them in the Center. As we get more and more involved in the unit, my students bring in their own books to add to the Center.

Memories of *Alice* in Wonderland

begin, as always, with memories. I tell my students my experiences with the story and they tell me theirs. Rarely do I find that they have had direct exposure to the book. More commonly, they have seen the Disney film or an adapted stage version. Sometimes they have performed in it themselves.

READING ALOUD ALICE IN WONDERLAND

Alice in Wonderland is best read aloud by an adult. Much of the book is dialogue which will be much more enjoyable for your students if you read it. The vocabulary is difficult and there are many Briticisms in the book. Reading it to your class means that they can focus on the content of the book rather than the mechanics of decoding. I encourage my students to follow along as I read, but whether or not you wish to do so depends on your particular class. What is most important is that the children get the sense of the humor and the language of the book.

I read from *The Annotated Alice* with notes by Martin Gardner. Much of the book is better appreciated with some background, and Gardner's notes are very comprehensive. For example, most of the poems are parodies of serious poems or songs of Carroll's day. Children in those days were expected to stand before adults and recite poems. Most of these poems taught lessons of good virtue. Thus, "How doth the little crocodile" plays wickedly with the most earnest poem "How doth the little busy bee." Reading a few stanzas of the original poem helps my students appreciate Carroll's humor. I point out some of the mathematical puzzles if the children seem agreeable. I am careful with these interruptions. Too many, and my students will lose interest in the story.

STUDYING THE ILLUSTRATIONS

I provide my students with many different illustrated editions of *Alice*. In addition to interruptions for context information, we also stop to study the different illustrators. The children become adept at noting the different approaches to illustrations very quickly. For example, Alice is represented in many different ways. Some illustrators keep to an Alice similar to Tenniel's. Others make Alice look more like photographs of the real Alice Liddell. Some doting fathers, like Barry Moser and Michael Hague, use their own daughters as Alice models. Also it is interesting to see what is actually illustrated. Since everything is so wild in Wonderland, some illustrators avoid certain scenes. Disney cut the Pig Baby out of his movie completely and his and others avoid the Duchess's kitchen, perhaps because beating a baby no longer seems particularly humorous. A number of illustrators have commented on contemporary issues within their drawings. Tenniel was a political cartoonist, and there is much speculation that certain characters are prominent politicians of his day. Ralph Steadman makes the playing cards into union cards, and Barry Moser has a March Hare that looks remarkably like Ringo Starr.

RESPONDING TO THE BOOK

I set aside a special *Alice* time every day for the class. Preparation includes washing hands as my students learn to handle the books as one does works of art. The books are from my own collection, and students are thrilled that I am allowing them to handle them. They have always taken very good care of my books. As we read we also discuss the book. Usually we review the previous day's reading before going on.

In any class, some children are more verbal than others. I ask my students to respond to the book in their journals as well as during class discussions. The journal responses often reveal that children who did not appear to be interested were actually quite engaged by the book.

QUESTIONS TO PONDER

nce I have finished the book I ask my students to answer the following questions in their journals.

How did you like the book?

Is it a fairy tale? Why or why not?

Is it like Cinderella? Why or why not?

Who was your favorite character and why?

Who was your favorite illustrator and why?

STUDENT JOURNAL RESPONSES TO THE BOOK

My feelings for the book have changed a lot. In the beginning I hated the story and plot, but now looking at it from a different point of view it is a very funny book. (especially the way Lewis Carroll writes it.)

Anna Monaco

Alice was a *great* story! I never knew it could be this good if you read it aloud. I have never read an unabridged version, but now I have all because you showed it to me.

Now I am almost finished with *Through the Looking-glass.* I think that both of these books are great. Although *Alice in Wonderland* I find a little better because Alice is doing more and finding more and more interesting things.

Jody Shechtman

CLASS DISCUSSIONS

Several class discussions follow, based on journal responses. I usually create a class chart such as the following during these discussions. This gives us a permanent record of the group's ideas about the book.

CLASS CHART ON *ALICE IN WONDERLAND*

Is it a fairy tale?

Yes, because it is magical;

you don't know it is a dream until the end;

it is unreal;

it is imaginative;

it is make-believe;

it has magical animals and magical people.

It is like *Cinderella* because:

The test was for Alice to get to the garden.

Alice has sisters and so does Cinderella.

The King and Queen act like Cinderella's stepmother.

The court case or croquet game is like Cinderella's "ball."

Alice and Cinderella are both girls.

There are animals in both stories.

Cinderella and Alice sometimes have similar personalities.

Favorite characters:

White Rabbit

Mock Turtle

Queen

Mad Hatter

March Hare

Cheshire Cat

Dormouse

Alice

Griffin

Hedgehog and Flamingo

Favorite illustrators:

Anthony Browne

William Bradley

John Tenniel

Mervyn Peake

Barry Moser

Lewis Carroll

DENNIS POTTER'S DREAMCHILD

*D*reamchild is a British film by Dennis Potter. It is a fictionalized account of a trip that Mrs. Alice Hargraves (nee Liddell) took to New York City on the centenary of Lewis Carroll's birth. Although Mrs. Hargraves did indeed travel to New York, most of the film is pure fantasy. It has the elderly Mrs. Hargraves trying to think back to her childhood and experiences with Lewis Carroll. At the same time she is haunted by characters from Wonderland. A subplot involves a romance between her young companion and a brash New York journalist.

STUDENT JOURNAL RESPONSES TO DREAMCHILD

I liked *Dreamchild* very much. I liked it because it wasn't so "kiddish." Some other "classic" movies I saw made me feel *sick.* Not because they were disgusting, it was because they were so *hammy.*

Eric Kiung

Dreamchild was great!

Recommended by me.

Enjoy the flashbacks.

Alice is confused because she doesn't understand.

Mrs. Hargraves is nice when you get to know her.

Charles Dodgson wants to marry Alice, but she doesn't realize it.

Happily, lively Alice doesn't take Mr. Dodgson seriously.

Interesting and makes you understand *Alice in Wonderland* better.

Lewis Carroll's real name is Charles Dodgson.

Does Alice start to understand at the end?

Rachel Rosenthal

DISNEY'S ALICE IN WONDERLAND

*L*ast year, for the first time, I decided to show the Disney film. It came up more often then usual in our discussions and I got a copy on sale.

The children were struck by how much of *Through the Looking-glass* was in the film. They also noted the great difference in the ending. In the book, Wonderland is clearly a dream while Disney's version has Alice running away from the court scene at the end. Disney's Wonderland is no dream.

STUDENT JOURNAL RESPONSES TO DISNEY'S *ALICE IN WONDERLAND*

I liked the movie a lot but they skipped my favorite parts, like the Mock Turtle. I would have liked to see what it would have looked like. They had her going through the looking-glass in the Disney version of *Alice in Wonderland.*

Disney had a good idea of mixing the two together to make one and it turned out pretty good. I especially liked the Walrus and the Carpenter in the Disney movie. In the movie I think Alice should have had brown or black hair because that's the way Lewis Carroll saw her and that's how she really looked (the real Alice Liddell.)

The idea of scrambling up sentences and making them go with different people (or should I say "things") was a good idea to make it shorter.

In all I liked them both a lot, the Disney movie and the Lewis Carroll version.

Mack Cauley

I really liked Disney's *Alice in Wonderland* because I think its really well fixed up for small children. Disney made half of the movie up because the wood doesn't have any of the ducks, vultures, momraths, or any of the other weird animals. Disney teaches a lesson and makes her seem grown up, but in Carroll he *doesn't* want Alice to grow up, because he wanted to marry her when she grew a little older.

Sarah Wertheimer

A CLASS COMPARISON OF CARROLL AND DISNEY

A class discussion focused on the similarities and differences between the book and the Disney film produced the chart on the following page.

ALICE PROJECT

he culminating project for this unit is for the students to do their own illustrations for the book. We talk about a variety of materials and ways to approach the project. Some children do a number of illustrations while others have preferred to create one large poster with many elements from the book. Those who feel that they can't draw have used collage and computer drawing programs to great effect. Last year two of my students created Wonderland stuffed animals. One was a most "cool" caterpillar and the other a delightful Cheshire Cat, with a caption from the story on his stomach.

Some of the most delightful written pieces have placed the Wonderland characters in different contexts. Thus, one child had Alice falling into a manhole in New York City. Another had her falling down an elevator shaft. In one child's view the Wonderland characters were all punk singers and the Duchess looked like Aretha Franklin.

CONCLUSION

Alice in Wonderland is a unique book within the canon of children's literature. Today, there are many who know it only from the Disney film and the actual book is often viewed as too difficult or strange for children today. Approaching the book through its many illustrators is a different way in, yet one that will yield many insights on the part of students and teachers.

CLASS CHART COMPARING CARROLL'S *ALICE* AND DISNEY'S *ALICE*

❀ Disney took poems and adages from one character and gave it to another. e.g. unbirthday from Humpty Dumpty to March Hare and Mad Hatter.

❀ Disney scene in woods seemed new although it referred to "Jabberwocky."

❀ Disney gives much more of a quest for Alice to go home while Carroll just has her trying to get to the garden.

❀ Disney's garden is very scary while Carroll's is interesting.

❀ Disney: Alice tries to wake up.

❀ Carroll: Sister wakes Alice up.

❀ Disney's is confusing because it mixes up two stories.

❀ Disney changes order of events and adds stuff.

❀ Disney left out the Duchess, the key into the garden, the Pig Baby, the Mock Turtle and Griffin.

❀ Disney added from *Looking-glass* Tweedledum and Tweedledee, unbirthday, talking flowers, Jabberwocky, woods

❀ Disney: Alice learns a lesson: no more nonsense. She seems older. Grows up during the movie. Wiser by the end. Is on a quest/journey.

❀ Carroll: There is no lesson. Not as serious. Alice is seven and a half. Carroll doesn't want her to grow up.

RECOMMENDED VIDEOS

Walt Disney's Alice in Wonderland. Walt Disney Home Video, 1991.

Dreamchild. Written by Dennis Potter. Directed by Gavin Millar. MGM/UA Video, 1992.

STUDENT PACKET

THE MANY FACES OF *ALICE*

INTRODUCTION

One of the most well known books ever written for children is *Alice in Wonderland*. It was written well over one hundred years ago in England yet remains remarkably popular all over the world. Just as fairy tales like *Cinderella* began as tales told by storytellers, so did *Alice in Wonderland* begin as a series of stories told by Lewis Carroll to Alice Liddell and her two sisters. Eventually, just as the most well known fairy tales were written down and published in books, so did Lewis Carroll write down his stories into what we now know as *Alice in Wonderland*. If you have not yet read (or heard) the real *Alice in Wonderland*, then you are in for a treat. It is imaginative, crazy, funny, clever, and wild all at the same time. Enjoy!

Our study of *Alice in Wonderland* will focus on the following:

❀ Pure enjoyment of the book!

I will read this book to you so you may read along if you wish or simply sit back and listen.

❀ A closer look at the puns, puzzles, and jokes in the book.

Lewis Carroll was a mathematician and threw in all kinds of puzzles in the book. He also loved puns (word plays) and making fun of popular activities of his day.

❀ The life and times of Lewis Carroll.

Lewis Carroll was a fascinating, brilliant man. In addition to being a scholar at Oxford University, he was a photographer and a minister.

❀ A close study of the many illustrators of *Alice in Wonderland*

While you may know the Tenniel illustrations best, you will be intrigued by the many other illustrators of the book. It is so well known that everyone seems to want to illustrate it. You will see how the book has been illustrated in different times, countries, and media.

LEWIS CARROLL

Lewis Carroll's real name was Charles Lutwidge Dodgson. He spent most of his life at Oxford University, England, teaching mathematics. Apparently he wasn't a great teacher; his classes were known to be dull and boring. Although we know him best as the author of the *Alice* books, he also wrote books about mathematics. Quite shy as an adult, he was most comfortable with children, especially little girls. Alice Liddell was his most famous child friend, but he had many throughout his life. He stuttered when nervous; perhaps that is why he seems to have been more comfortable with children than adults. In addition to writing mathematic books and creating fantasy stories, Lewis Carroll enjoyed photography. Many of his photos of child friends remain. Certainly, there are many of Alice Liddell.

After the publication of *Alice in Wonderland* and *Alice Through the Looking-glass*, Carroll wrote other books for children. Unfortunately, they were not as good as the *Alice* books and are only of interest to Carroll scholars today.

Lewis Carroll died on January 14, 1898.

THE CREATION OF *ALICE IN WONDERLAND*

Alice in Wonderland began as a story told on a boat trip. Lewis Carroll and his friend, the Reverend Robinson Duckworth, took the three Liddell girls out on the Thames River on July 4, 1862. The three girls were Lorina, age thirteen, Alice, age ten, and Edith, age eight. Carroll wrote about the expedition in his diary and later added a note that it was then that he had told the story of Alice's adventures underground.

Alice so enjoyed the story that Carroll decided to write it down for her. (Remember, this was before typewriters or computers.) He finally presented her with *Alice's Adventures Underground* on November 26, 1864. The book was beautifully handwritten with illustrations by Lewis Carroll himself.

Before Carroll gave the book to Alice, he showed it to some friends who felt he should publish it. So he revised the book, changed parts, added parts, and found John Tenniel to do the illustrations. The book we know today, *Alice in Wonderland*, came out in 1865. It was a huge success. Before long it was known throughout the world. There are people today who collect Alices from all over the world. One collector had *Alices* in 125 different languages!

ILLUSTRATORS OF *ALICE IN WONDERLAND*

The very first illustrator of *Alice* was Lewis Carroll himself. Since he was not a professional illustrator, when he decided to publish the book he looked for a well-known illustrator. John Tenniel was a well-known cartoonist; *Alice* was his first children's book. Carroll worked closely with Tenniel to see that the illustrations were just as he wanted them. Tenniel also illustrated *Alice Through the Looking-glass.* Throughout Lewis Carroll's life, he and Tenniel were the only published illustrators of the book.

After Lewis Carroll died, other well-known illustrators attempted to illustrate the book. One of the first, Charles Rackham, was already well known. Over the years, many others have attempted to illustrate the book. Alice has been presented as a nineteen twenties flapper, as an African-American, and as an Australian aboriginal. Every artist who takes on Wonderland makes it their own. Hopefully, you will too.

MEMORIES OF *ALICE IN WONDERLAND*

What do you know of this book? Perhaps you saw the Disney cartoon or acted in a play version? Did you ever read it or have it read to you? Perhaps you just vaguely know about it; that's just fine too. Write down what you know of *Alice in Wonderland* here.

_____

_____

_____

_____

_____

_____

_____

_____

_____

READING
ALICE IN WONDERLAND

I will read this book to you. You will listen or follow along in the different illustrated editions. We will need to rotate the different versions through the class so everyone has a chance to look at them. It is important to handle these books carefully. Begin with clean hands and be careful as you turn pages. They are works of art and deserve your gentle care.

As I read the book to you, we will stop the reading when necessary to look at illustrations, to consider why different artists made the choices they made regarding what they illustrated and didn't and how they illustrated parts of the book. We will also interrupt the reading to discuss the puzzles and jokes in the book. How often we stop will depend on what the class wishes. For example, if the class would rather wait till the end of a chapter before looking at all the illustrations, that is what we will do. Each class I've done this unit with has its own way of doing it. I will respect the way this particular class wishes to approach the reading, the observing of references and illustrations, and the discussion.

RESPONDING TO
ALICE IN WONDERLAND

You will be asked both during and at the end of the readings to respond in your journal to the book and whatever comes up in discussions as we study the text and the illustrations.

QUESTIONS TO PONDER
AFTER READING
ALICE IN WONDERLAND

How did you like the book?

_____

_____

_____

_____

_____

Is it a fairy tale? Why or why not?

_____

_____

_____

_____

_____

Which character did you like best and why?

_____

_____

_____

_____

_____

Which illustrator did you like best and why?

_____

_____

_____

_____

_____

_____

_____

FINAL *ALICE IN WONDERLAND* PROJECT

Now that you have seen what all those other artists did, you are going to do your own illustrations of *Alice in Wonderland*! Think carefully about what scenes you want to illustrate, what materials you wish to use, etc. Be creative and have fun! Remember not only all the different ways this book has been illustrated, but all the ways traditional fairy tales are approached by writers, filmmakers, and artists. Your path is wide open!

BOOK INTO FILM: A Comparative Study of *The Wonderful Wizard of Oz*—Baum's Book and the MGM Movie

*...I've done a good deal of thinking,
these past three years, about the advantages
of a good pair of ruby slippers...*

SALMAN RUSHDIE
*BFI FILM CLASSICS:
THE WIZARD OF OZ*

elevision came to my house when I was eight. Even after it was ensconced in our guest room, my sister and I were strictly limited to one hour a day. In order to squeeze in as many programs as possible we left the room for commercials. The way we figured it, that gave us three programs.

The one hour rule was lifted for special events such as the yearly showing of *The Wizard of Oz*. That was an event I looked forward to and savored long after it was over. The T.V. was black and white so the dramatic switch to color when Dorothy got to Oz was lost to me. It didn't matter, though. I adored it. No other movie had the same effect on me as a child.

Today, my students have a different relationship with television and movies. Zapping from program to program, "surfing" the sixty-plus cable channels, everything is just the push of a remote control button away. If they like a movie they can rent it or buy it, and view it as often as they wish. Certainly, the dramatic special effects of *The Wizard of Oz* can seem tame in this day of computerized morphing and digitization. Yet, even for these children, *The Wizard of Oz* movie still enthralls. It is part of our popular culture. Who hasn't heard or said, "I don't think we are in Kansas anymore" or "There's no place like home." Reading, viewing, and studying the film and the original text is fascinating for children, as well as an excellent way to have them consider how a story is transformed in different media.

An American Fairy Tale

Frank Baum wanted *The Wonderful Wizard of Oz* (published in 1900) to be a new kind of fairy tale. He also made it distinctly American. Dorothy is a farm girl from Kansas, and Baum brilliantly contrasts the plain prairies with the extravagant landscapes of Oz. The traditional European fairy tales were full of class issues—princes marrying peasant girls, clever farmers becoming kings and the like. Wealth was often the reward. Baum, ever the American, turned away from such issues. No one marries in the book and no one seems very interested in royalty or gaining wealth. The Wicked Witch of the West is the ogre of the story, but Dorothy's only reward for killing her is to go home, to the very same drab, spartan Kansas farm she left at the beginning. She does not go back with material wealth, only with a greater appreciation of her love for her aunt and uncle and their simple life.

Metro-Goldwyn Mayer's 1939 Film

Early film versions of the book were unsuccessful and forgettable. The MGM film was different. The studio was interested in creating a blockbuster movie, something to compete with Disney's first full-length animated feature, *Snow White and the Seven Dwarfs*. The combination of memorable musical comedy numbers, sterling performances, and special effects made the movie the classic it is today.

A reasonable success when first released, the movie really became known to all due to its television showings in the fifties and sixties. Today, most Americans know the story from the movie, not from the book.

Wizard of Oz Memories

This unit begins, as do all my units, with a discussion of the children's background knowledge of the book and film. Most of the children know the film, far fewer know the book. Often they have performed a theatrical version in school or camp. They love to discuss what they know of the movie.

One year I had a student who was reading a number of scary books. He and I were having a wonderful time discussing the books and scary stories in his journal. At one point he mentioned that he and his mother were reading a book together which was so scary that she finished it on her own after he went to bed. I responded that I was always so easily scared as a child that I doubt that I would have been able to read the book. I went on to describe my tremendous fear of Oz's flaming head in the MGM movie. My student was flabbergasted that this scared me. It was mighty tame stuff in his opinion. Today with the level of violence and terror so heightened in film and television, nine year olds can be hard pressed to find witches and flying monkeys particularly scary.

The Book

READING THE BOOK

The Wonderful Wizard of Oz is a book that my fourth graders can read on their own. Baum is a serviceable writer; the content of his book is much more interesting than his actual writing. I have my students read a facsimile version published by Dover so that they can also experience Denslow's original illustrations.

Many of my students find this book one of their favorites of the year. They are fascinated by the landscape of Oz, and the story holds them even if they already know it from the movie. I frequently have children reading through lunch and at every available free moment. It has been especially rewarding to see students who do not normally speak positively about reading talk about "loving" this book. It is a sure-fire hit every time.

DISCUSSING THE BOOK

During *The Wizard of Oz* unit, I always ask my students how they want to handle discussions. Do they want to have whole class discussions? Smaller groups? Discuss the book as they read or after they are finished? This is a unit we do well into the school year, and I want them to begin to make such decisions, not me. Generally, my students have felt as I have: that a whole class discussion is great because everyone gets to hear everyone's great ideas. On the downside, children get to speak less in a large group. While I prefer to discuss a book once everyone has completed it, my students often prefer to discuss it as they read it.

Last year my class decided they wanted to meet in half-class groups so that they could talk more. We met several times as the groups read the book (they wanted to start the discussion before finishing the book). After several meetings, the class asked to have the groups be reformed so that they could hear other children's thoughts about the book.

By this time in the school year my students are well versed in critical analysis. They love to look for connections to other books, to mull over unusual questions. One boy noted that the silver slippers (ruby in the movie) were like Cinderella's glass slippers. I found this a fascinating comment since Dorothy seems so unlike Cinderella in other ways. Yet, Baum did place the all important magic in those shoes, just as the shoe test in the *Cinderella* tale is all important to her ultimate happiness.

Another child commented that she didn't think the Wicked Witch was really wicked, just greedy. The others in the group animatedly agreed. I was very interested in this idea and tried to see if it was because she didn't kill people. The children were unable to define wickedness for me, only to keep insisting that the witch wasn't.

These kinds of comments always stay with me, and I like to bring them up with different groups of children to see if they agree, disagree, or have variations to bring to the ideas. I will certainly ask next year's class whether they think the silver slippers are like Cinderella's glass slippers and whether they think the Wicked Witch is really wicked.

STUDENT JOURNAL RESPONSES

Students wrote journal responses during and after reading the book. We brainstormed entry ideas, and many were particularly interested in comparing the book to *Alice in Wonderland*.

> I like it a lot but I thought it would be a lot different because I've seen the movie so many times and the movie is very different. I think Dorothy and Alice have totally different personalities. Alice is very curious and when she saw the shoes (the silver slippers) she'd probably say something like "Oh what curious things. They are very beautiful. I wish Dinah (her cat) was here. She'd tell me if I should try them on." Dorothy is kind of straight foreword. Also, if Alice was called a sorceress she'd be like "How fun it must be to be a sorceress but I'm not one. . . ."
>
> Eli Meltzer

. . . These are a couple of comments I have on both stories: I think that there was a big difference on how rich or poor Dorothy and Alice were. It is obvious that Dorothy's family was not rich. I think Alice was more wealthy because she went to school and everything (lessons.) I also think that Dorothy does not have as much character as Alice. But maybe Alice needed more logic to survive in Wonderland.

Eric Kiung

I think *The Wizard of Oz* is very different from *Alice in Wonderland* because Alice just wants to get to the garden because she thinks its pretty and Dorothy is more reliable because she worries about her aunt and uncle and getting home. I myself like Dorothy better because she isn't selfish like Alice. I like *The Wizard of Oz* better than *Alice in Wonderland* because I like quests and Dorothy is on a quest to find the Wizard of Oz.

Sarah Wertheimer

The Wizard of Oz is really good so far, especially when the bad witches die. The Wicked Witch of the West just died in my book. Now they're going back to the Wizard! I've read the book many times and would say that this time it is the best. I can't wait to see what the end of the book is like again!

Jody Shechtman

I think *The Wizard of Oz* is really great! I like Dorothy better than Alice because she's more common. She seems to care about people more and isn't as bossy as Alice. She is kind of like Wilbur in *Charlotte's Web*. She is humble and doesn't think that much of herself. She

thinks everyone is better, nicer, and smarter than her. She seems to deserve a nice land better than Alices does. Since Alice is bossy and can be *VERY* rude, she doesn't deserve all of her adventures other than the one with the queen. It should have taught her a lesson, but all it did was make her even more bossy and self defensive. Dorothy is very sensitive to other people's feelings and isn't ever rude (at least not so far.) I'm really enjoying the book. I can't wait to see what happens. I think its *very* well written. It pulls you in and makes you feel like you're there. I never know that it was such a good book. This is the best book I've read in a *LONG* time.

Rachel Rosenthal

CHARACTER DESCRIPTIONS

I know that there will be times in my students' educational future where they will be expected to respond to books in more formal ways such as plot summaries, character descriptions, or a setting map. I use *The Wizard of Oz* to expose them to this kind of writing. We brainstorm the kinds of things that would go into a character description. Sometimes we discuss organizing a character description into two parts: a physical description and a personality description.

Dorothy is a very kind hearted girl. She is so sweet that when she heard she killed the witch she was terrified for she had never in her life killed anyone. Dorothy likes Oz but she wants to get home to her aunt and uncle because she is afraid they will be worried. Dorothy is also very sensitive. She also worried about everything. She keeps her troubles to herself especially when she is with her companions.

Alexandra Saltiel

Dorothy is a very young person not very capable of going outside alone. She is very kind and sweet. Dorothy is very little, is not very smart, and is always thinking of home. She can get very scared at times so she goes on journeys with friends that support her. Her personality is very different. She is very sweet and kind if you hurt yourself then she would try to help you or panic. My example of Dorothy: Dorothy would be able to do lots of things but she really hates *death*. When Dorothy gets mad she really doesn't get that mad because she isn't that kinds of person.

Anne Kurtz

THE FILM

Usually my students have seen the movie before. However, they approach the class viewing very differently after having read the book since it is so different from the movie. Whole sections from the book have been eliminated, Dorothy is much older in the movie, and the whole story is framed as a dream Dorothy has after being knocked out during the tornado. For Baum's Dorothy, Oz is quite real. Certainly, the children enjoy analyzing the similarities and differences between the book and the movie as well as their likes and dislikes.

STUDENT RESPONSES AFTER VIEWING THE MGM MOVIE

After the children have had sufficient time to read, discuss, and respond to the book, we view the movie. If possible, I recommend either the Fiftieth Anniversary Edition video or the new Collector's Edition. Both have footage of outtakes, home movies, newsreels, and other material related to the movie. My children have especially enjoyed the extended sequence of the Scarecrow's "If I Only Had a Heart." The cut portion includes the Scarecrow flying across the cornfield!

Once we have viewed the movie we discuss it and compare it to the book. We also often compare it to more current movies, in terms of scariness and special effects.

I liked both the movie and the book. I think that there were a couple of things about the movie that did not make sense like the Cowardly Lion. The Cowardly Lion never got part of his wish, which was to be the "king of the beasts. . . ." Another part that did not make any sense to me was the part in the movie when Dorothy was riding in the cyclone and saw those people flying by in the window. How could an old lady be knitting when she was in a cyclone? (see picture below)

Eric Kiung

I liked the book better than the movie because the book had more detail. The movie cut out a lot. I can't really blame them, but they cut out a lot of the best parts and they also put in some things that weren't meant to be there. It was like they wrote a whole new book that was only based on *The Wizard of Oz*. They had ruby slippers instead of silvers ones, there was only one good witch and it was all just a bad dream. Also, Dorothy was *much* older. I think I will keep on reading the Oz books. We chose the right time to read the book. I was just in a Purim play called *Follow the Hamatash Road*. I was a Winkie and I did the "Yo Hee Ho" march. It was fun!

Rachel Rosenthal

CREATING FANTASY LANDS: A PROJECT

riting fantasy is tough. It requires the creation of a convincing land, sympathetic characters, and an exciting narrative. Adult writers struggle with it as much as child writers do. Yet children love to write fantasy, almost as much as they like to read it. Too many teachers discourage this kind of writing because it easily disintegrates into simplistic, lengthy, video game-type stories. I know because I was one of those teachers! For years, my students would come to me proudly with twenty-page fantasy stories based on the latest video game or movie. Invariably they would get lost in their stories and would quickly finish it up with: "And then she (or he) woke up." And that would be that. The child author was proud of the story and unprepared to revise, and I was hard pressed to respond to something that had lost me after the first battle (pages five through ten.) Most of these stories involved detailed descriptions of the fantasy land, a remarkable number of characters with special powers, and battles galore.

Then several years ago I developed a way of using classic fantasy tales as models for my young writers. After completing our studies of *Alice in Wonderland* and *The Wizard of Oz,* I suggested that interested students try to develop their own stories of children like themselves traveling to a fantasy land, meeting a series of memorable characters, and finally coming home. Rather than beginning with the narrative, I suggested that they begin with the land.

The children had a great time creating elaborate lands. Many drew complex maps of them. Some of my students were happy to stop then while others moved on to create characters and ultimately a story. The revelation for me, was that all the stories did not have to be finished. Whether a child simply described a fantasy land or created a whole story didn't matter. The important thing was that they had good models to follow, and they did as much or as little as they wished. Those that decided to publish their stories were interested and willing to do the necessary revisions and final editing.

Writing fantasy is unwieldy, but that is no reason to throw it out of the writing workshop. Giving children good models to truly study will help them gain control of the genre as they craft their own stories.

Benjamin Pickard, author of the story excerpts on pages 92 and 93, was a great fan of Lewis Carroll's and Brian Jacques's works.

CONCLUSION

The Wizard of Oz is the most American of literary fairy tales. Well known to us through the MGM film, it is a delightful story for children to explore. Contrasting such a well-known film to the original book is an excellent way to develop children's analytic abilities. Additionally, it is a fine model for those children interested in creating their own fantasy worlds.

Chapter 1—THE PARTY

"HAPPEE BIRTHDAAY TOOO YOOOOO!" Will blew mightily and the candles went out.

"I WANT CAKE! I WANT CAKE!" screamed Ben, Will's younger brother.

"It's Will's birthday and he gets the first slice," said Mrs. Stevenson, Ben and Will's mom.

"Mmmm . . . this is goood cake!" said Will, happily anticipating the presents he was about to get.

When everyone had filled themselves with cake, Will's Mom announced that it was time for the presents. "Open mine first," said Ben. Will opened it. It was a G.I. Joe figure! "I'm going to play with it. Okay, Will?"

"Fine," said Will, not surprised. (It was the same thing last year, except with He-Man.) "Now, I'll open Mom's," said Will. It was a hyper-super-ultra train set. Will had expected to get it, but it was still exciting.

Just then Will's Dad walked in. "Here's your gift!" he said.

"Come on! Open it!" said Ben, back with an anxious look on his face and a certain permanently immobilized action figure in his hand.

Will took one look at the parcel and ripped it open. Inside was a box with holes punched in it. It moved. "Is it a hamster?" asked Will. A questioning oink (actually an "inkoay") proved him wrong. "It's a pig," said Will excited.

"A Latin pig," said his father.

* * *

Will snuggled into his pillow. Will took a closer look at the animal. It had pink hair, unlike his and his brother's which was a mousy brown, but its eyes were brown like his.

He was about to fall asleep when he heard a gentle, but firm voice saying, "IAY EEDNAY OTAY AKETAY OUYAY OTAY YMAY ORLDWAY." Then, with a firmer sound, Will heard, "HOMUS PORJUS CASTLEUS FLYUS!" Suddenly Will felt woozy and dropped off.

The following excerpt from Richard Zbeda's story, "William in Robotland" shows the direct influence of Lewis Carroll.

Chapter 3—THE CRICKET

The Cricket's house was just like a regular house except there were no places to sleep in. This was very confusing to William and he was sure to ask about it when they were inside, having tea, all settled in and had settled down. Then William saw his chance and asked, "How come there are no beds?"

"What are beds?" asked the Cricket.

"Why they're the things you sleep on at night," replied William.

"What are they like?" asked the Fly.

"Well they're sort of like cushions," replied William.

"Well we don't sleep," said the Cricket and the Fly.

"That's funny" thought William, "I think everybody should sleep."

"Everybody sleeps but us," said the Fly. "It's always so boring on Sundays."

"There is never anything to do," said the Cricket.

"But what about other days?" asked William.

"What do you mean?" asked the Cricket.

"Why, when everybody is asleep on regular days," replied William.

"Here the others don't sleep on regular days, just on Sundays," said the Fly. . . .

Then there was silence for a few minutes. Finally William said, "I should be getting on now."

But the Cricket and the Fly were not listening, and the Cricket said, "I'm going to recite my favorite poem. Here, it is."

How doth the gentle Parakeet,
improve its colorful wings,
flies beautifully through the air beautifully and clear,
he's very much fit for a king.

How cheerfully he seems to chirp,
how neatly he spreads his tail,
and when the cat starts to look,
he's gone and left no trail.

THE WIZARD OF OZ: Book into Film

INTRODUCTION

The Wizard of Oz is America's fairy tale. Many many years ago, L. Frank Baum decided to write a modern fairy tale. He felt that traditional fairy tales like "Cinderella" were old-fashioned and that it was time for someone to write some new ones. So he wrote the ever-popular Oz stories. Today we know them best because of the 1939 MGM movie. Judy Garland as Dorothy, the ruby slippers, and "Over the Rainbow" are what we think of when we think of Oz.

We will begin by reading L. Frank Baum's *The Wizard of Oz*. After our initial reading, we will investigate Baum and consider how and why he wrote the Oz books. In our roles as literary scholars, we will also compare *The Wizard of Oz* to other well-known fantasies such as *Alice in Wonderland*. Next we will view the 1939 movie, investigate its creation, and compare it to the original book. By the end of the unit, you should all be Oz-experts!

L. FRANK BAUM

L. Frank Baum was born in Chittenango, New York in 1856. He worked as a salesman, a playwright, and a journalist before becoming a writer of children's books. His first great success was *Father Goose, His Book*, a collection of poems illustrated by W. W. Denslow. *The Wizard of Oz*, with illustrations by Denslow, was published in 1900. It was a tremendous success right away. Eventually, many other Oz books were also written, but *The Wizard of Oz* has always been the most well known.

Baum had been thinking about writing a fairy tale for some time. The Oz stories began as bedtime stories for his children and their friends which Baum then wrote into an early draft titled "The Emerald City." His publishers disliked the title because they were fearful that a book with a jewel in the title wouldn't sell. Other titles under consideration were "From Kansas to Fairyland," "The Fairyland of Oz," and "The Land of Oz."

The *Wizard of Oz* came out in 1900, two years after Lewis Carroll's death. While *The Wizard of Oz* is quite different from *Alice in Wonderland*, they are often compared. It seems likely that Baum was familiar with Carroll's work and was trying to create his own imaginary land with a girl heroine.

Baum wrote thirteen more Oz books as well as stage versions of the stories. He died at Ozcot, his Hollywood home, on May 6, 1919.

MEMORIES OF *THE WIZARD OF OZ*

Some of you may already know something about the story. If you have had some experience with the story, please write about it below. You may have seen a movie version, read the book, had it read to you, or performed in a camp version of the story.

_____

_____

_____

_____

_____

_____

_____

READING THE BOOK

We will decide as a class how to read the book. This might mean dividing into smaller discussion sections with due dates decided by these groups. Keep in mind that we are a reading community, and some of us will complete the book before others. This may be because some of us are faster readers. It may also be because some of us will get so wrapped up in the story that we will read nonstop until we reach the last page. Others of us may read less quickly or less intensely. You should all be sensitive to each other and remember that each of us has his/her own style of reading that must be respected. It is like eating a cookie—some of us gulp it down while others of us nibble it—both ways are valid and enjoyable!

RESPONDING TO THE BOOK

We will respond to the book in many ways:
- ❁ in reading journal entries.
- ❁ in small group discussions.
- ❁ in whole group discussions.

QUESTIONS TO PONDER
AFTER READING THE BOOK

How did you like the book?

_____

_____

_____

Who was your favorite character? Why?

_____

_____

_____

_____

_____

Do you note any similarities and/or differences to other books you have read?

_____

_____

_____

_____

_____

_____

_____

_____

THE METRO-GOLDWYN-MAYER MOVIE

While there were several earlier Oz movies, the 1939 MGM one is the most well known. No expense was spared in making this movie. A great search was made for the perfect Dorothy; even the highly popular Shirley Temple was considered for the role. Eventually sixteen-year-old Judy Garland was selected even though Dorothy is described in the book as a much younger child.

The movie story is quite different from the book. Whole chapters were left out and, most notably, Oz becomes Dorothy's dream. The result is a very different story from Baum's.

QUESTIONS TO PONDER
AFTER VIEWING
THE MGM MOVIE

How did you like the movie?

_____

_____

_____

_____

_____

_____

Who was your favorite character in the movie? Was it the same as your favorite character in the book?

_____

_____

_____

_____

_____

_____

_____

How did it compare to the book?

_____

_____

_____

_____

_____

_____

_____

_____

_____

CHAPTER 7

Reading Fantasy Literature Aloud

"What about a story?" said Christopher Robin.
"What about a story?" I said.

A. A. MILNE
WINNIE-THE-POOH

typical day in my classroom: writing workshop has just ended. Children are busy, putting away folders, tying shoes, going out for drinks, admiring someone's new eraser. There is the sound of productive bustle; these children know exactly what they are doing. Before long someone has turned out the light. Now children are getting pillows and stretching out on the rug. One takes her special place under my desk; others stay at their own desks, some in seats, others sprawled on top. A few sit as close to me as possible, at my feet, leaning against my chair, seated on my desk. Soon it is quiet. I open the book. Story time has begun.

I have always loved being read to. There was my father, sitting by my bed, reading the vain attempts of a cat to half talk in Edgar Eager's *Half Magic*. Or my prim sixth grade teacher, facing us in our rows, as she read the next chapter of *Born to Trot*. I could have read those books on my own, of course, but there was something different and special about having them read to me. Recently, at a restaurant, a good friend spent most of the meal regaling me with his favorite parts of Dave Barry's latest book. I may read the book on my own at some point, but listening to my friend so gleefully reading was an equally pleasurable experience. However old we are, listening to someone read is always delightful. And while all kinds of written material can and should be read aloud in classrooms, fantasy literature, which began in the words of storytellers and the oral tradition, is a particularly suitable vehicle for story time.

STORY TIME

All schoolchildren should have a daily read aloud time, a time when all they have to do is sit and listen. This should be a time separate from any academic time, a time devoted to reading aloud. Some schools do this first thing in the morning, sometimes even with a reading over the school-wide intercom system. Others may individualize it more in different classrooms by inviting students to read or creating regularly ongoing story time. Often story time is under the auspices of the librarian. Unfortunately, too many of us associate story time with little children, or see it as too babyish for, say, fourth graders. Scheduling daily read aloud time with appealing books is worthwhile at any grade level.

THE RITUAL OF READING ALOUD

Ralph Peterson, in his book *Life in a Crowded Place* (1992), writes of the importance of ritual in school. We all know about that. The way we start our day, a roll call or the Pledge of Allegiance, the way we begin and end math period or gym, all involve rituals. A story time ritual helps set the right tone for listening. Teachers have many different rituals for story time. I have heard of teachers who use a candle to set the mood, lighting it for the duration of the reading. Some have special areas of their classrooms designated for story time; others have a special chair they sit in while reading aloud. Whatever ritual you establish in your classroom should be yours, but it should exist. Story time should be seen as a separate, special time, just as important as all the other times in the school day.

STORY TIME ETIQUETTE

When I read to my students, I expect them to be still, to be silent, and to listen. Drawing may be a way to listen for some children, but for too many others it is a way of not listening, or of interacting with a neighbor (looking at his drawing, borrowing the right crayon, and the like). I would strongly advise establishing a community of listeners, one where the expectation is that everyone is doing nothing other than listening to the story and thinking about the story. Sometimes it helps to ask children to review what they heard the day before, or to have them discuss elements in the story during and after the reading. However, I only use such methods to help children with their primary task which is to enjoy the story. Questions should be used cautiously. Too many, and the children will become bored. In a read aloud time, the story is all important. Rituals, questions, and the like are only ways to keep the story at center stage.

BOOK SELECTION

Book selection for story time needs to be a balance of teacher input and student suggestions. I generally present more than one book to my class and ask them to vote. If I begin a book and sense that the class is not enjoying it, I will ask for another vote. There is no point plugging on with a read aloud selection if you have lost your audience. Books that work for one group of children may not work for another.

I select books that I like, that read aloud well, and that correspond to the interests of the particular group of children I have at a given time. I purposely read books that are not related to our other academic studies. Thus, when we study *Cinderella*, I read

Cinderella stories during our language arts period and something else during story time. When we study the Hopi, I read their myths during social studies time, not during our special read aloud time. I think it is important to make the story time separate, with its own requirements, its own book list, and activities. Teachers need to see story time as a worthwhile part of the day, one that deserves attention and a curriculum of its own.

While I enjoy fantasy literature and read aloud a lot of it, I also read aloud other kinds of literature. I stick to fiction, but I could certainly see reading biography or autobiography if that was the interest of that particular class and teacher. My students are always big fans of animal stories. Phyllis Reynolds Naylor's *Shiloh* is always a sure hit. Realistic fiction is also worthwhile. Another fine read aloud, one that straddles the realistic and fantasy genres, is Jerry Spinelli's *Maniac Magee.* Both these books have the kind of strong narrative voices that make them especially good as read alouds.

Some points to consider when selecting a fantasy book to read aloud:

1. An exciting narrative is important. I read aloud for about fifteen to twenty minutes, and I can usually read a chapter in that time. Leaving my audience in suspense until the next day is a great part of reading aloud. It makes my students anticipate with delight the next day's reading. Selecting books that have dramatic events is important. A book that meanders along, such as *Alice in Wonderland*, does not work particularly well for most groups of children.

2. Interesting characters that children can relate to are important. I have a particular fondness for stories where ordinary children come across magic. Much of the humor in such books occurs when these children deal with magic and magical beings. If the characters are animals or imaginary characters like dragons, they still need to have human traits that children can enjoy. Roald Dahl's books are full of such characters. While *The Wind in the Willows'* characters are animals, they are so human in their foibles that children can easily identify with them.

3. Well-developed dialogue is important. The reader can read different characters in different voices. Too much description can bore a young audience.

4. Children who are not good listeners can be won over with humor. I usually start my story program with humorous books. John Sczieska's *The Stinky Cheese Man and Other Fairly Stupid Tales* is a perennial hit.

RESPONDING TO READ ALOUDS

My students respond to read alouds by their silences (the contented kind that means they have truly enjoyed the reading), by discussions, and by journal entries. Most of the books I read are chapter books, stories that take several weeks to complete. We usually start our story time by reviewing the previous day's reading. I keep this review short, detailed only enough to be sure everyone knows what has happened. Sometimes, if it seems appropriate, I let students guess what will happen next. They like that! At the end of the day's reading, we sometimes reflect on what has happened in the story. Again, I keep this brief. It is important that story time not become a listening skills time; that is, it shouldn't be a time to make children feel they are being tested. It should be a pleasurable time—all questions and discussions should be done as a means of enhancing not deadening the enjoyment of the read aloud.

Journals are a good way to extend the story time. I always invite my students to respond to the read aloud in their journals. Occasionally, if I want to get a more detailed sense of how they feel about a particular book, I might assigned them a response to the book. I did this recently with *The Boggart,* a recent book by Susan Cooper.

I really think that *The Boggart* is a really good read aloud. When you were first reading the book to us I didn't think the book was all that great but then one day I started to really enjoy it. Today when you stopped I'm really just in suspense.
Anne Kurtz

I like *The Boggart* because of all the tricks that the Boggart plays. Also, I think the book is written well. You can *see* what is happening. Can the Boggart talk? The author never did make the Boggart say anything so far. I think in the end, the Boggart will go back to the castle.

Eric Kiung

EXPRESSIVE READINGS

There is certainly a skill in reading aloud. My students love different voices for different characters, a raise in my voice and a quickening in tempo at a particularly exciting part of the story. Consider reading aloud as a performance. Just as you are performing when you are teaching a lesson, so you are when you are reading aloud. You need to make it exciting, scary, funny—whatever the book calls for. It is the reader's responsibility to the text, to the author, and to the audience to keep the book alive through his or her performance.

CONCLUSION

Reading aloud to a group of children is a very intimate experience. I find that a special relationship develops between me and my listeners. At its best, a story time should be like a bedtime reading, like the special time that parents and children have together with a book. When that happens with my class and me, I can ask for nothing more. It can be magical when we finish a book, to sit quietly, thinking how perfect a book it was.

REFERENCES

Milne, A. A. (1926). *Winnie-the-Pooh.* New York: Dutton.

Peterson, Ralph. (1992). *Life in a Crowded Place.* Portsmouth, NH: Heinemann.

Fantasy Literature in an Independent Reading Program

And when the firemen turned off the hose and were standing in the wet, smoky room, Jim's aunt, Miss Prothero, came downstairs and peered in at them. Jim and I waited very quietly, to hear what she would say to them. She said the right thing always. She looked at the three tall firemen in their shiny helmets, standing among the smoke and cinders and dissolving snowballs, and she said: "Would you like anything to read?"

DYLAN THOMAS
A CHILD'S CHRISTMAS IN WALES

I'm a New Yorker, which means I occasionally take the subway. Due to a propensity towards carsickness I can't read. However, most of my fellow passengers do read, no matter how crowded, hot, dirty, or noisy the train is. The diversity of reading material is remarkable. I see thrillers, classics, magazines, textbooks, memos, newsletters, romances, and mysteries. I love looking over someone's shoulder at a Russian newspaper, trying to figure out the headlines. Tourists seriously study guidebooks as they scramble out to view the sights. How great to live in a city of readers!

I want my students to be lifelong readers; to read for enjoyment and pleasure, not merely to pass a test or to get the latest stock report. I want them to be the kind of people who take lots of books on vacation, who enjoy browsing in a bookstore, who read on public transportation. To develop such a temperment, children must not only read a lot, but have plenty of opportunities to select their own reading material. Just as each child is an individual, so are their book choices highly personal. There are children who lean toward sports stories while others adore realistic animal sagas. Some are series aficionados, still others prefer informational texts. And finally, there are the fantasy buffs, lovers of other worlds and magical beings.

Making Independent Reading Important

In a classroom like mine, where independent reading coexists next to whole class literature studies, it is critical for me to reinforce the importance of independent reading constantly. Students need to know that their own choice in reading has just as much value as the reading being done with the whole class. Some students may prefer their own book choices to the group choices. It is important for such children to have the opportunity to make their own selections, while maintaining the group work as well. At the end of the year, when I ask children to identify their favorite books, there will be an even split between those they read for group literature study and those they read for independent reading. Time and validation for choice reading is an important part of my language arts program.

Structuring Independent Reading

 From the first day of school, I make it very clear that the most important homework expected for my class is the half hour of nightly reading. This is not considered something to do in addition to regular homework—it *is* "regular homework." Parents and I work together with children helping them find books they like, a good place to read, a way to plan reading. At first, reluctant readers need lots of help with this assignment. But I have found that with parent support most of my fourth graders become far more comfortable with the assignment as the year goes on.

I keep track of students' independent reading via individual conferences, journal entries, and group discussions. I must admit that I struggle to find time to see my students often for individual conferences. With all the other work going on, these reading conferences are not as frequent as I would like. My students and I enjoy them, a few minutes just to chat about a book. I always just ask the student to tell me what they are reading, how they like it, what they plan to read next, if they want any help from me.

Most of my interaction with my students and their independent reading centers around their journals. I schedule a weekly journal time. We talk about possible journal entries. I sometimes ask students to read favorite journal entries to the group, and then the students use the remainder of the time to write their entries. If children are too brief I set a time requirement: they must write for ten minutes, for example. I feel a time requirement works much better than word or page length. If children know they must write for a certain amount of time they usually begin thinking of something to write about.

Journal Responses to Independent Reading

As the year goes on and my students become more adept at making literary connections, they enjoy finding ties between independent reading and group literature books. The following journal excerpts demonstrate the different ways my students select books, read at home, and respond to their reading.

> I just finished reading *James and the Giant Peach* for the tenth time, but it's still one of my favorites. Now I've read all of Dahl's children's books except *The Twits*, but I plan on reading it as soon as possible. I hear it's really funny. I seem to have a strange habit of always eating a peach

whenever I read it!

Rachel Rosenthal

I really like the *Half Magic* series even though I'm not done with it. So far I've read four of the books. I like the *Half Magic* series because the books just take me to another land. It's as if I'm the person that the adventure is happening to. What I really like that occurs in all of Edgar Eager's books is that you know as much as the characters know. I mean, he doesn't tell you things the characters don't know. All I know is that I really like his books.

Sarah Wertheimer

At home I'm reading *The Lion, The Witch, and the Wardrobe.* I read it last year, but I wanted to read it again because my mom gave it to me, it was fourth grade level, so I thought I might want to read it again, because I might not have understood all of it. . .*The Lion, the Witch, and the Wardrobe* is very serious. It has nothing funny. It is sort of like Cinderella because at first the four kids in the beginning were just regular kids. Then in the end the kids become kings and queens. The book seems to go by very slow. In *The Wizard of Oz* the book goes by very fast and you enjoy it a lot more too because it has a story with a lot of action...

Richard Zbeda

I'm reading *A Wrinkle in Time.* I started on Monday. The first time I saw the book I thought it was going to be about aliens. I think I know why, because the cover is a little weird. But then as it came to a surprise to me that it had normal people and that they lived in a normal house and they went to a normal school. I think the way the author started the book was interesting. What I thought was a sort of good way to start off the book was that they couldn't find their father. One of my favorite characters is Charles Wallace because he always knows how Meg is feeling and what she wants. Something that I feel is not good about Meg is that when she gets mad or frustrated is that she blames it on somebody and gets into a fight.

Anne Kurtz

I'm reading *The B.F.G.* and I really like it because it is funny and I've never heard of a Big Friendly Giant. I read it to Sean and Erin, my sisters, and they liked it because one of the main characters in the book is Sophie and I have a cousin named Sophie. They also liked the idea of a Big Friendly Giant and I like it when he's catching dreams the most.

I'm not all the way done but close.

Mack Cauley

I am reading *Dealing With Dragons.* My favorite characters in the book are the dragons. I think it is because it is interesting how human like they are. I like it because it is funny and the wizards are dumb. I like this kind of book. There is a guy who is minding his own business, but then he either wants to or does something spectacular. Like *The Trumpet of the Swan.* Louis is dumb and wants to speak (or trumpet.) His journey takes place because he has to repay the trumpet his father stole.

Eric Kiung

CONCLUSION

I have noticed over the years that certain kinds of fantasy books seem especially appealing for independent reading. These are books that may be too long and complex for a group study, or too idiosyncratic for many children. Yet, these are books that children adore on their own.

REFERENCE

Thomas, Dylan. (1984). *The Collected Stories*. New York: New Directions Books.

Bibliography

CHAPTER 1

Bettelheim, Bruno. (1989). *The Uses of Enchantment: The Meaning and Importance of Fairy Tales.* New York: Vintage.

Blatt, Gloria (Ed). (1993). *Once Upon a Folktale: Capturing the Folklore Process with Children.* New York: Teachers College Press.

Lurie, Alison. (1990). *Don't Tell the Grown-Ups: Why Kids Love the Books They Do.* New York: Avon.

Sale, Roger. (1978). *Fairy Tales and After: From Snow White to E. B. White.* Cambridge, MA: Harvard University Press.

CHAPTER 2

Calkins, Lucy. (1986). *The Art of Teaching Writing.* Portsmouth, NH: Heinemann.

Graves, Donald. (1991). *Build a Literate Classroom.* Portsmouth, NH: Heinemann.

Harwayne, Shelley. (1991). *Lasting Impressions: Weaving Literature into the Writing Workshop.* Portsmouth, NH: Heinemann.

Moss, Joy F. (1990). *Focus on Literature: A Context for Literacy Learning.* Katonah, NY: Richard C. Owens.

Rosenblatt, Louise M. (1983). *Literature as Exploration.* New York: Modern Language Association.

Sloan, Glenna Davis. (1991). *The Child as Critic: Teaching Literature in Elementary and Middle Schools.* New York: Teachers College Press.

CHAPTER 3

Elledge, Scott. (1984). *E. B. White: A Biography.* New York: W. W. Norton and Company.

Gherman, Beverly. (1992). *E. B. White: Some Writer!* New York: Atheneum.

White, E. B. (1994). *The Annotated Charlotte's Web.* Illustrated by Garth Williams. Introduction and Notes by Peter F. Neumeyer. New York: Harper Collins.

CHAPTER 4

Everytime I go into a bookstore I find another *Cinderella*. These are some of my favorites.

Ahlberg, Janet and Allan. (1986). "Cinderella." In *The Jolly Postman*. Boston: Little Brown

Brooke, William J. (1990). "The Fitting of the Slipper." In *A Telling of Tales*. New York: Harper and Row.

Brown, Marcia. (1954). *Cinderella*. New York: Macmillan.

Carter, Angela. (1981). "Cinderella: or, The Little Glass Slipper." In *Sleeping Beauty and Other Favorite Fairy Tales*. Illustrated by Michael Foreman. Boston: Joshua Morris.

Climo, Shirley. (1989). *The Egyptian Cinderella*. Illustrated by Ruth Heller. New York: Crowell.

Climo, Shirley, (1993). *The Korean Cinderella*. Illustrated by Ruth Heller. New York: Harper Collins.

Cinderella. Facsimile of 1859 shape book. Chester, CT: Applewood Books.

Delamare, David. (1993). *Cinderella*. New York: Green Tiger Press.

Dijs, Carla. (1991). *Cinderella*. New York: Dell Yearling.

Easton, Samantha. (1992). *Cinderella*. Illustrated by Lynn Bywater. Kansas City: Andrews and McMeel.

Edens, Cooper. (1991). "Cinderella." In *The Three Princesses: Cinderella, Sleeping Beauty, Snow White: The Ultimate Illustrated Edition*. New York: Bantam Books.

Erlich, Amy. (1985). *Cinderella*. Illustrated by Susan Jeffers. New York: Dial.

Evans, C. S. (1987). *Cinderella*. Illustrated by Arthur Rackham. London: Chancellor Press.

Garner, James Finn. (1994). "Cinderella." In *Politically Correct Bedtime Stories*. New York: Macmillan.

Hooks, William H. (1987). *Moss Gown*. Illustrated by Donald Carrick. New York: Clarion Books.

Huck, Charlotte. (1989). *Princess Furball*. Illustrated by Anita Lobel. New York: Greenwillow.

Jackson, Ellen. (1994). *Cinder Edna*. Illustrated by Kevin O'Malley. New York: Lothrop, Lee & Shepard.

Karlin, Barbara. (1989). *Cinderella*. Illustrated by James Marshall. New York: Little Brown.

Martin, Rafe. (1992). *The Rough-Face Girl*. Illustrated by David Shannon. New York: G.P. Putnam's Sons.

Minters, Frances. (1994). *Cinder-Elly*. Illustrated by G. Brian Karas. New York: Viking.

Myers, Bernice. (1985). *Sidney Rella and the Glass Sneaker*. New York: Macmillan.

Perlman, Janet. (1992). *Cinderella Penguin or The Little Glass Flipper*. New York: Viking.

Perrault, Charles. (1974). "Cinderella." In *The Classic Fairy Tales*. Iona and Peter Opie (Eds.) New York: Oxford University Press.

Perrault, Charles. (1972). *Cinderella or the Little Glass Slipper*. Illustrated by Errol Le Cain. New York: Viking Penguin.

Perrault, Charles. (1991). "Cinderella." In *The Sleeping Beauty and Other Classic French Fairy Tales*. Illustrated by W. Heath Robinson. New York: Children's Classics.

Pienkowski, Jan. (1977). *Cinderella*. New York: Alfred A Knopf.

San Jose, Christine. (1994). *Cinderella*. Illustrated by Deborah Santini. Honesdale, PA: Boyds Mills Press.

San Souci, Robert D. (1989). *The Talking Eggs*. Illustrated by Jerry Pinkney. New York: Ballantine.

San Souci, Robert D. (1994). *Sootface*. Illustrated by Daniel San Souci. New York: Doubleday.

Scieszka, Jon. (1992). "Cinderumpelstiltskin." In *The Stinky Cheese Man and Other Fairly Stupid Fairy Tales*. Illustrated by Lane Smith. New York: Viking.

Sierra, Judy. (1992). *The Oryx Multicultural Folktale Series: Cinderella*. Phoenix: Oryx Press.

Shorto, Russell. (1990). *Cinderella*. Illustrated by T. Lewis. New York: Birch Lane.

Steptoe, John. (1987). *Mufaro's Beautiful Daughters*. New York: Lothrop, Lee & Shepard.

Storey, Rita. (1992). *Cinderella*. Illustrated by Amelia Rosato. London: Puffin Books.

Walt Disney's Moving Picture Flip Book. B. Shackman and Co.

Wegman, William. (1993). *Cinderella*. New York: Hyperion.

Winthrop, Elizabeth. (1991). *Vasilissa the Beautiful*. Illustrated by Alexander Koshkin. New York: HarperCollins.

CINDERELLA MOVIES

These are all available on video.

Ashpet: An Appalachian Folktale. Directed by Tom Davenport, 1989.

Cinderella. Directed by Wilfred Jackson. Disney Studios, 1949.

Cinderella. Directed by Charles S. Dubin. Based on Rogers & Hammerstein's 1957 musical. Samuel Goldwyn, 1964.

Cinderella. Written by Mark Curtiss & Rod Ash. Directed by Mark Cullingham. Executive producer Shelley Duvall. Platypus Production, 1984.

Cinderfella. Written by Frank Tashlin. Directed by Jerry Lewis. Paramount, 1960.

Cindy Eller. Directed by Lee Grant. 1985.

The Glass Slipper. Written by Helen Deutsch. Directed by Charles Walters. 1955.

La Cenerentola. A 1981 production of Gioacchini Antonio Rossini's opera with Frederica Von Stade at La Scala in Milan.

Mutzmag: An Appalachian Folktale. Directed by Tom Davenport, 1992.

My Fair Lady. Screenplay by Alan Jay Lerner. Directed by George Cukor. Produced by Herman Levin, from the Lerner and Loewe musical. Warner Brothers, 1964.

Pretty in Pink. Produced and directed by John Hughes. Paramount, 1986.

Pygmalion. Directed by Anthony Asquith & Leslie Howard. 1938.

CINDERELLA RESEARCH

Aarne, Antti, and Stith Thompson. (1961). *The Types of the Folktale.* 2nd rev. ed. Folklore Fellows Communications no. 184. Helskinki: Academia Scientariarum Fennica.

Cox, Marian Roalfe. (1893). *Cinderella; 345 Variants.* London: David Nutt.

Dundes, Alan. (1988). *Cinderella: A Casebook.* Madison, WI: The University of Wisconsin Press.

Moss, Joy F. (1990). "Cinderella Tales: A Multicultural Experience." In *Focus on Literature: A Context for Literacy Learning.* Katonah, NY: Richard C. Owen, pp. 167–185.

Philip, Neil. (1988). *The Cinderella Story.* London: Penguin.

Rooth, Anna Birgitta. (1951). *The Cinderella Cycle.* Lund: C.W.K. Gleerup.

Tatar, Maria. (1992). *Off With Their Heads! Fairy Tales and the Culture of Childhood.* Princeton, NJ: Princeton University Press.

Zipes, Jack. (1987). *Don't Bet on the Prince: Contemporary Feminist Fairy Tales in North America and England.* New York: Routledge.

CHAPTER 5

Recommended Illustrated Editions of *Alice in Wonderland*

Carroll, Lewis. (1985). *Alice's Adventures Underground.* Illustrated by the author. London: Pavilion Books Limited and the British Library.
> This is a facsimile edition of the manuscript Lewis Carroll wrote for Alice Liddell. It is worth having on hand to compare to the later published version.

Carroll, Lewis. (1988). *Alice's Adventures in Wonderland.* Illustrated by Anthony Browne. New York: Knopf.
> This is always one of my students' favorite editions. Browne is the author/illustrator of many well-known picture books such as *Gorilla*.

Carroll, Lewis. (1992). *Alice's Adventures in Wonderland.* Retold by David Blair. Illustrated by John Bradley. Philadelphia: Running Press.
> This is a large, oversized book with bold, active illustrations well liked by my students.

Carroll, Lewis. (1993). *Alice's Adventures in Wonderland.* Retold by David Blair. Illustrated by Graham Evernden. Philadelphia: Running Press.
> This is a miniature edition that my students have enjoyed handling.

Carroll, Lewis. (1982). *Alice's Adventures in Wonderland.* Illustrated by Barry Moser. New York: Harcourt Brace Jovanovich.
> The illustrations in this edition are all woodcuts. They are certainly very dark. Moser is the most adult oriented of any illustrator in my collection.

Carroll, Lewis. (1989). *Alice's Adventures in Wonderland.* Illustrated by Arthur Rackham. London: William Heinemann Ltd.
> Rackham was an illustrator in the early part of this century known for many classics such as *Cinderella*. He was the first prominent illustrator to try *Alice* after Tenniel, and some critics did not treat him kindly.

Carroll, Lewis. (1993). *Alice's Adventures in Wonderland.* Abridged and illustrated by Tony Ross. London: Andersen Press.
> Tony Ross is a popular British illustrator. These are very lively, appealing drawings.

Carroll, Lewis. (1988). *Alice's Adventures in Wonderland.* Illustrated by John Tenniel and Bessie Pease Gutmann. Children's Classics.
> An inexpensive edition. Gutmann's Alice is very young and innocent looking.

Carroll, Lewis. (1991). *Alice's Adventures in Wonderland.* New York: Dell Yearling.
> A pop-up book illustrated by Jenny Thorne after Sir John Tenniel.

Carroll, Lewis. (1988). *Alice's Adventures in Wonderland.* Illustrated by Justin Todd. London: Lynx.
> This is well-liked by my students.

Carroll, Lewis. (1989). *Alice's Adventures in Wonderland and Through the Looking-Glass.* Illustrated by Marketa Prachaticka. Chicago: Wellington Publishing.
    These are beautiful, highly original drawings.

Carroll, Lewis. (1960). *The Annotated Alice.* Illustrated by John Tenniel. Introduction and notes by Martin Gardner. New York: Meridian.
    This is an extremely useful text to have on hand. The notes are excellent.

Carroll, Lewis. (1986). *The Complete Alice and The Hunting of the Snark.* Illustrated by Ralph Steadman. London: Jonathan Cape Ltd.
    Difficult to find, but terrific. I bought this copy in England some years ago. Steadman is a cartoonist and his drawings are wild and witty.

Carroll, Lewis. (1990). *More Annotated Alice.* Illustrated by Peter Newell. Notes by Martin Gardner. New York: Random House.
    A beautiful edition. The Newell drawings are delightful. His Alice is a sleek, long-haired child, very different from Tenniel's.

Carroll, Lewis. (1966). *The Nursery "Alice."* Illustrated by John Tenniel. New York: Dover.
    My students have always gotten a kick out of this, Lewis Carroll's own adaptation for very young children.

Carroll, Lewis. (1989). *The Ultimate Illustrated Alice's Adventures in Wonderland.* Compiled and arranged by Cooper Edens. New York: Bantam.
    If you can only get a couple of different editions, make this one of them. It is full of illustrations by many different artists. Gives a fine overview of all the different approaches to the illustration of this book.

Carroll, Lewis. (1993). *Walt Disney's Alice in Wonderland.* New York: Mouse Works, Penguin Books.
    A recent version of the film.

Goldberg, Whoopi. (1992). *Alice.* New York: Bantam Books.
    This is a wild story based on Wonderland characters. Great illustrations.

Rayher, E. (1982). *Alice's Flip Book.* New York: Merrimack Pub. Corp.
    A little flip book of the Cheshire Cat, disappearing and reappearing.

Sheppard, Nancy. (1992). *Alitji in Dreamland.* An aboriginal version of Lewis Carroll's *Alice's Adventures in Wonderland.* Illustrated by Donna Leslie. Berkeley: Ten Speed Press.
    An aboriginal retelling with striking artwork.

ALICE IN WONDERLAND RESEARCH

Bjork, Christina. (1993). *The Other Alice: The Story of Alice Liddell and Alice in Wonderland.* Illustrated by Inga-Karin Eriksson. Translated by Joan Sandin. Stockholm: Raben & Sjogren.
    Excellent source of information on the real Alice and Lewis Carroll.

Hacher, Michael. (1985). *The Tenniel Illustrations to the "Alice" Books.* Ohio State University Press.
For anyone especially interested in the Tenniel illustrations.

Hudson, Derek. (1976). *Lewis Carroll: An Illustrated Biography.* London: Constable.
A good biography of Lewis Carroll.

CHAPTER 6

Baum, L. Frank. (1973). *The Annotated Wizard of Oz.* Introduction, notes, and bibliography by Michael Patrick Hearn. Illustrated by W. W. Denslow. New York: Clarkson N. Potter.

Baum, L. Frank. (1960). *The Wonderful Wizard of Oz.* Illustrated by W. W. Denslow. New York: Dover.

Baum, L. Frank. (1986). *The Wonderful Wizard of Oz.* Illustrated by Barry Moser. Berkeley: University of California.

Carpenter, Angelica Shirley, and Jean Shirley. (1992). *L. Frank Baum: Royal Historian of Oz.* Minneapolis: Lerner Publications.

Eyles, Allen. (1985). *The World of Oz.* New York: Viking Penguin.

Rushdie, Salman. (1993). *BFI Film Classics: The Wizard of Oz.* London: British Film Institute.

CHAPTER 7

The following are fantasy books that I have found read aloud especially well.

Babbit, Natalie. (1974). *The Devil's Storybook.* New York: Farrar Straus Giroux.
A collection of stories involving the Devil's efforts to make mischief on earth.

Babbit, Natalie. (1969). *The Search for Delicious.* New York: Farrar Straus Giroux.
A search throughout a kingdom for the true meaning of the word *delicious.*

Bellairs, John. (1973). *The House with a Clock in Its Walls.* New York: Dial.
A highly suspenseful book involving a mystery and the supernatural.

Cooper, Susan. (1993). *The Boggart.* New York: Margeret K. McElderry Books.
An exciting book mixing a very contemporary pair of Canadian children with a very ancient Scottish spirit. Computers and magic mix in a delightful and dramatic way.

Dahl, Roald. (1961). *James and the Giant Peach.* New York: Knopf.
A very beloved book by this highly popular author. James, a mistreated little boy, grows a magical peach and ends up having fabulous adventures because of it.

Eager, Edgar. (1954). *Half Magic*. New York: Harcourt Brace Jovanovich.
   Four children find a magical coin that grants wishes that only come half true. The results can be messy and hilarious.

Grahame, Kenneth. (1940.) *The Wind in the Willows*. New York: Heritage.
   A beautiful book about Mole and his good friends Rat and Toad and their experiences along the riverbank.

Kipling, Rudyard. (1978). *Just So Stories*. New York: Crown.
   A delightful collection of stories that were originally written by Kipling for his children.

MacDonald, Betty. (1957). *Hello, Mrs. Piggle-Wiggle*. New York: Harper Trophy.
   Mrs. Piggle-Wiggle, an eccentric little lady, lives in an upside down house and does magical cures for kids.

Milne, A. A. (1926). *Winnie-the-Pooh*. New York: Dutton.
   The amusing and warm adventures of Pooh Bear and his assorted friends, all stuffed animals of Christopher Robin.

O'Brian, Robert. (1971). *Mrs. Frisby and the Rats of NIMH*. New York: Scholastic.
   Mrs. Frisby, a mouse worried about her son's illness, seeks out the super-smart rats of NIMH for help.

Pinkwater, Daniel. (1977). *Fat Men from Space*. New York: Dodd, Mead and Co.
   William's tooth suddenly becomes a radio and receives warnings of an invasion from outer space. Pinkwater's books are strange, yet funny in a deadpan sort of way.

Tolkien, J. R. R. (1966). *The Hobbit*. Boston: Houghton Mifflin.
   A timid little hobbit is corralled by the wizard Gandalf to help a group of dwarves to kill the dragon Smaug and get their kingdom back.

Wrede, Patricia. (1990). *Dealing with Dragons*. San Diego: Harcourt Brace Jovanovich.
   Cimorene hates being a regular princess so she runs off to be a dragon's princess. Keeping dumb princes from rescuing her are the least of her problems as wizards become difficult.

CHAPTER 8

This bibliography was compiled and annotated with help from the following members of my 1994–95 fourth grade class: Jamie Bass, Eric Benson, Meredith Blank, Kate Bregman, Emily Chinitz, Christopher Cirgenski, David Coen, George Davis, Evan Goldblatt, Jessica Greenbaum, Emily Horbar, Gregory Kress, Anna Kwawer, Ashley Newman, Kelty Niles, Sam Raboy, Robert Russell, Kate Turner, Dana Weisman.

The following books are a sampling of the many fantasy books available for children. I have tried to provide a range suitable for children of varying interests and reading levels.

Alexander, Lloyd. (1964). *The Book of Three.* New York: Holt, Rinehart and Winston.
   Taran, an Assistant Pig-Keeper, goes on a grand adventure to save his land from evil. The first in a series.

Butterworth. Oliver. (1956). *The Enormous Egg.* New York: Dell Yearling.
   Nate Twitchell's chicken lays an enormous egg that hatches a dinosaur. Now he and his friends have to learn how to care for an ever-growing dinosaur.

Coville, Bruce. (1991). *Jeremy Thatcher Dragon Hatcher.* New York: Harcourt Brace Jovanovich.
   Jeremy, a kid who is teased at school, finds a mysterious egg at a store. The dragon that hatches from the egg changes his life.

Coville, Bruce. (1989). *My Teacher Is an Alien.* New York: Simon & Schuster.
   Did you ever think of your teacher as an alien? Well, if so this book is for you!

Dahl, Roald. (1964). *Charlie and the Chocolate Factory.* New York: Knopf.
   Every child's dream happens to Charlie Bucket—a visit to the greatest chocolate factory in the world.

Dahl, Roald. (1988). *Matilda.* New York: Viking.
   Matilda is a very tiny genius child with special powers. She never gets mad, she gets even (especially with her evil headmistress, the Trunchbull).

Dahl, Roald. (1982). *The BFG.* New York: Farrar Straus Giroux.
   A story about a little girl and a big friendly giant whose career is catching dreams.

Edwards, Julie. (1974). *The Last of the Really Great Wangdoodles.* New York: HarperCollins.
   Three siblings meet a famous Nobel prize winning professor who takes them on a magical adventure to Wangdoodleland.

Gannett, Ruth Stiles. (1948). *My Father's Dragon.* New York: Knopf.
   The narrator is a boy telling about his father's adventures with dragons.

Gurney, James. (1992). *Dinotopia.* Atlanta: Turner.
   This is about a young boy and his father who are shipwrecked and end up in a mixed-up world of dinosaurs and humans working together.

Howe, James. (1979). *Bunnicula.* New York: Avon.
　　Chester, the exaggerating cat; Harold, the scaredy-dog; and Howie, the puppy, solve
　　mysteries involving Bunnicula, the vampire bunny.

Jones, Diana Wynne. (1977). *Dogsbody.* New York: Greenwillow.
　　This book involves a fantasy creature called a luminary who gets into big trouble and
　　has to go to Earth in the form of a dog to retrieve the Zoi.

Juster, Norton. (1961). *The Phantom Tollbooth.* New York: Random House.
　　This is about a bored boy who goes through a magical toy tollbooth into all kinds of
　　imaginary lands. It is a particularly fun book for kids who like playing with words and
　　numbers.

L'Engle, Madeline. (1962). *A Wrinkle in Time.* New York: Dell Yearling.
　　This book is about Meg, a brave girl, her little brother Charles Wallace, and her kind
　　friend Calvin and how they defeat the dreaded IT by traveling through space and
　　time.

Lewis, C. S. (1950). *The Lion, the Witch and the Wardrobe.* New York: Macmillan.
　　A little girl and her sister and brothers travel through a wardrobe to the land of
　　Narnia. There they have many adventures trying to defeat the White Witch. This is
　　one of the Chronicles of Narnia.

Lofting, Hugh. (1988). *The Story of Doctor Dolittle.* New York: Dell Yearling.
　　Dr. Dolittle was a people doctor who becomes an animal doctor who can talk their
　　languages. This is adapted slightly from the original to eliminate some racist
　　elements.

Nesbit, E. (1985). *Five Children and It.* New York: Puffin.
　　A story about five children who find a magical being who gives them a wish a day. Of
　　course the wishes never turn out quite as they hope!

Norton, Mary. (1952). *The Borrowers.* New York: Harcourt, Brace and World.
　　Arrietty, Pod, and Homily are Borrowers, a bunch of small people who "borrow"
　　things from people. In this book, the first of a series, they search for a new secure
　　home.

Pene Du Bois, Robert. (1947). *The Twenty-one Balloons.* New York: Viking.
　　The eccentric Professor Sherman takes off in a balloon trip around the world. His
　　trip is cut short by an accident and he ends up on a most unique island.

Rogers, Mary. (1972). *Freaky Friday.* New York: Harper and Row.
　　Have you ever wished to turn into your mother? It happens to Annabel Andrews.
　　The results are less than expected but hilarious for both mother and daughter.

Sachar, Louis. (1978). *Sideways Stories from Wayside School.* New York: Avon.
　　This is a school that was built sideways—one classroom on top of another instead of
　　next to each other and no nineteenth floor. Such an unusual building has unusual
　　kids, teachers, and happenings.

Selden, George. (1960). *The Cricket in Times Square*. New York: Dell Yearling.
Mario's parents run a newstand in Times Square. It is there that he comes across Chester, the cricket; Tucker, the Broadway mouse; and Harry the Cat.

Steig, William. (1972). *Dominic*. New York: Farrar Straus Giroux.
The adventures of a brave dog named Dominic and his dealings with the Doomsday Gang.

Thurber, James. (1950). *The Thirteen Clocks*. New York: Simon and Schuster.
A witty story about a prince who hates being a prince, becomes a minstrel, and saves the Princess Saralinda from the cold cold duke.

Winthrop, Elizabeth. (1985). *The Castle in the Attic*. New York: Bantam.
William's baby-sitter gives him a toy castle as a going away present before she is to return to England for good. It mysteriously comes to life and William goes on an adventure inside.

Wrede, Patricia. (1991). *Searching for Dragons*. New York: Harcourt Brace Jovanovich.
Mendenbar, King of the Enchanted Forest, and Cimorene, Chief Cook and Librarian for the King of the Dragons go searching for a missing dragon.

Yolen, Jane. (1988). *The Devil's Arithmetic*. New York: Viking.
This is fantasy mixed with history as the heroine is transported back in time to experience the horrors of the Holocaust first hand.

Yolen, Jane. (1981). *Sleeping Ugly*. New York: Coward-McCann.
Neither Princess Miserella nor Plain Jane end up quite as expected though each gets what she deserves.

Notes

Notes

Notes

Notes

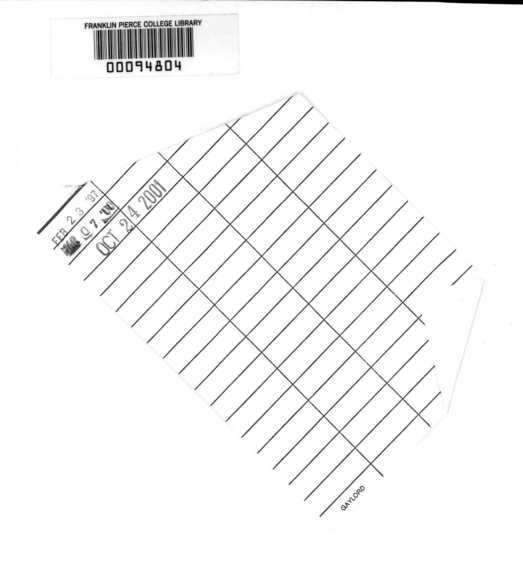